MY
TRUTH

MY
TRUTH

by EDDA MUSSOLINI ÇIANO
as told to ALBERT ZARCA

Translated from the French by Eileen Finletter

WILLIAM MORROW AND COMPANY, INC.
NEW YORK   1977

B
Ciano

French edition published by Editions Stock under the title *Temoignage pour un homme* © 1975, Editions Stock.

Printed in the United States of America.

1   2   3   4   5   6   7   8   9   10

Library of Congress Cataloging in Publication Data

Ciano, Edda Mussolini, Contessa.
   My truth.

     Translation of Temoignage pour un homme.
     Includes index.
     1. Ciano, Edda Mussolini, Contessa.
2. Statesman's wives—Italy—Biography.
3. Ciano, Galeazzo, Conte, 1903-1944. 4. Statesmen—Italy—Biography. 5. Mussolini, Benito, 1883-1945. 6. Italy—Politics and government—1922-1945. I. Zarca, Albert. II. Title.
DG575.C516A3513   1977   945.091'092'4 [B]
ISBN 0-688-03099-8

BOOK DESIGN   CARL WEISS

MY
TRUTH

I

Verona, January 11, 1944, at about nine o'clock in the morning. A gray, pallid dawn threatening foul weather dimly lit the cold, almost empty streets of this city in Northern Italy.

An Italian army minibus passed through the gates of Scalzi prison and continued toward the outskirts of the city, escorted by motorcyclists belonging to the militia as well as by two official cars.

Approximately ten minutes later the procession arrived at its final destination, Fort Procolo. It entered the fort and came to a stop at the shooting range not far from a small hill enclosed within a high wall. Twenty or more armed militiamen were waiting there along with four or five German officers, several of whom were carrying cameras.

Six persons descended from the bus: a priest, whose black silhouette stood out against the grayness of the landscape, and five men dressed in plain clothes.

The first of these, a fragile old man, conservatively dressed in a dark suit, wearing a black hat and sporting a white goatee, looked around, then took several steps in the direction of the priest. He was Emilio de Bono, one of the earliest of Mussolini's comrades-in-arms, who had been by Il Duce's side when he came to power on October 30, 1922. Bono is listed in the annals of history as one of the *quadrumviri* who were invested with total military powers during the March on Rome. After having occupied several important posts in the Fascist regime, he became a field marshal of Italy.

His lips were moving in silent prayer, for only half an hour earlier Emilio de Bono, having been condemned to death by a Fascist tribunal for "treason," had received the last rites and learned that he was going to die.

The second person to appear wore a raincoat and a gray hat. He walked with a firm step, his hands thrust into his pockets, and he stared impassively at the faces surrounding him. Only his pallor and his tightened jaws betrayed his nervous tension. He was Galeazzo Ciano, and he too was aware that his steps were leading him toward death. But, contrary to his four companions, he had known for several days that there was no hope for a reprieve. Although he had been Benito Mussolini's right-hand man for nearly ten years, one of his closest collaborators, considered by some to be his heir, he too had been condemned to death for "treason." In addition, for fourteen years he had been Il Duce's son-in-law.

Three other men followed Bono and Ciano: Luciano Gottardi, president until 1943 of the Confederation of Industrial Workers; Carlo Pareschi, Minister of Agriculture and Forests until July 25, 1943; and Giovanni Marinelli, who had occupied several posts within the Fascist party and in the government, notably as Undersecretary of the Postal and Telegraph Service.

Although Gottardi and Pareschi appeared calm despite their strained faces, Marinelli could not overcome the legitimate terror that had assailed him ever since he had been informed that he was going to die. His steps faltered and his jailers literally had to drag him toward the place of execution. Bono, Ciano, Gottardi, and Pareschi knew that they were going to die because on July 24, 1943, they had voted yes to a resolution that in part disavowed Il Duce, presented by Dino Grandi at the last meeting of the Fascist Inner Council, but Marinelli had never understood this. His deafness had practically prohibited him from following the debates at that meeting, so that he had believed he was obeying Mussolini in voting for the Grandi resolution; and he had understood almost nothing at the trial during which he had been condemned to death along with the others.

Within several minutes Verona, which had once enjoyed its hour of glory as a rich independent republic and an important commercial crossroads, was to enter once more into history, this time as the background to a drama that would mark one of the turning points of Fascism. That drama was to become not only one of the most notorious but also one of the least explicable events of the Second World War.

A group was formed, composed of the five condemned men preceded by Don Chiot, the prison chaplain, Signor Cosmin, the prefect—who was to die several weeks later of a pulmonary congestion—two or three militia officers, a judge, a doctor, and a journalist. Close by were five chairs, legs thrust into the ground, awaiting those who were going to die.

The photographers loaded their cameras, and several film cameras began to turn. The militiamen who made up the execution squad, dressed in black trousers, gray-green vests, and black caps, were lined up in two rows—the first kneeling, the second standing behind them.

The small group stopped beside the chairs. One of the army officers signaled to the condemned men to sit down. They straddled the chairs, their backs turned toward the firing squad because, according to Italian law, "traitors" must be shot in the back.

It was approximately twenty minutes past nine in the morning. The militiamen tied the wrists of the condemned men to the back of their chairs. Before holding out his wrists, Galeazzo Ciano beckoned to Prefect Cosmin to approach and whispered several words to him; then Gottardi took off his coat and scarf and asked that they be given to his son.

A profound silence reigned over the shooting range. Then one of the officers read the sentence and the list of reasons that had led the judges to pronounce the verdict. When the voice had stopped, Bono could be heard praying.

Suddenly a cry arose. It was the voice of Marinelli, shouting, "Don't shoot! Don't shoot!"

At the same moment Galeazzo Ciano turned his head and fixed his eyes intently on the militiamen who were preparing to shoot.

The commander, Nicola Furlotti, lowered his arm, and the rounds were fired.

Bono slumped over the back of his chair, instantly killed. The others rolled on the ground with cries of agony. A second round finished them off. Only Galeazzo Ciano still lay groaning.

Nicola Furlotti rushed to his side, accompanied by Dr. Caretto, the medical expert. Furlotti held his revolver to Ciano's temple and shot, but that was not enough. He shot a second time, and finally Galeazzo Ciano stopped breathing. It was over.

The bodies of the executed "criminals" were transported to a mortuary chapel in Verona and exposed to the public to prove that there had been no substitution of persons—particularly that Galeazzo Ciano was truly dead. The victims were rapidly buried under a thick coverlet of flowers by the inhabitants of Verona—which was their way of showing their sympathy, their pardon and, perhaps, their remorse.

Fifteen months and seventeen days later, on April 28, 1945, Benito Mussolini, in whose name these men had been executed, fell in turn under the bullets of Walter Adusio, alias "Colonel Valerio," a Communist whom he had not only rescued from deportation after receiving a pleading letter from Adusio's mother, but for whom he had found work in a Fascist agricultural cooperative.

Thirty years later I was shown a photograph depicting Galeazzo Ciano staring at his executioners, taken at the very instant when the execution squad fired. That photograph was the genesis of this book.

Why did it make such an impression on me when there exist so many others, sometimes more terrible, of so many other crimes committed for the sake of one or another idea?

First, because the five men executed that day were Fascists, proclaiming their fidelity to Mussolini but killed by Fascist bullets in the name of Mussolini.

Then, because the trial during which they were judged was, to my mind, dominated by fanaticism, masquerading under the guise of reasons of state, rather than by a sense of equity and respect for the principles of justice. After all, Mussolini himself denied the trial any moral value and disputed the political advantages of the sentence pronounced in his name.

Third, because, independently of its political consequence due to the persons involved, the trial at Verona and the death of

Ciano were part of a human tragedy whose principal actors played major roles on the international scene: Mussolini, his wife Donna Rachele, his favorite daughter Edda and her husband Galeazzo Ciano, Hitler, Himmler, Ribbentrop, Kaltenbrunner, the dress designer Emilio Pucci, who almost lost his life helping Edda Ciano, priests, to name only the major figures. And then there were more obscure persons, unknown even thirty years later, who had involuntarily or not been implicated in this drama and who had chosen to be silent, while others exaggerated their declarations more to justify themselves or to boast of the part they had played than to serve the cause of truth.

Finally, because the central figure of the tragedy, Galeazzo Ciano, seemed to me very different from the portrait depicting him in the accounts that I had read. I suspected that certain traits had been concealed, certain features emphasized, usually to his disadvantage or, at least, to give weight to a preconceived version of history.

His last moments invited reflection—why, for example, did he turn his head around to face the firing squad at the moment of his death?

Could this gesture have been the reflex of a man of only forty who understandably wanted to live and who, despite what he knew, might have believed in a last-minute miracle, for example, a pardon that Edda, his wife and also Il Duce's daughter, might finally have extracted from her father?

Or had he perhaps hoped to be saved in extremis by a German commando group under the orders of General Harster, commanding officer of the S.S. at Verona, who had been entrusted with the task of liberating him? This seems unlikely, since he had probably been informed that Himmler and Kaltenbrunner, who had promised to have him liberated in exchange for his notebooks, had been forced to renounce their project because of an intervention by Ribbentrop and on the order of the Führer, who had confirmed his veto by personally telephoning General Harster.

It is extremely likely that it was a gesture of bravado by a man who wished to look death in the face rather than have it strike him in the back, a fact that had been haunting him ever since his arrest.

"I feel the balls enter my back and pierce the nape of my neck while I sleep," he had said one day to a friend and fellow prisoner. "What a horrible sensation! I shall not be able to endure being executed," he had added, "but I shall not give those who wanted my death the pleasure of seeing me die a coward."

No one, and with good reason, will ever be able to answer these questions with any precision. But in the gaze of that man who was going to die there was an indescribable something of such grandeur and nobility that I was incited to try to learn more about him than I already knew.

And so I set to work. But the picture of Count Ciano that began to emerge, a quite different one from that I had previously known, soon overflowed the canvas to include a portrait of Benito Mussolini himself, a Mussolini divergent from the image represented by history, whose ascendancy over those who surrounded him made it possible to better understand Galeazzo Ciano's tragedy as well as Mussolini's own.

I was also able to place Count Ciano in the world in which he lived, to situate him properly for the first time. This helped me to understand his psychological formation and thus the motives for his acts. I discovered what some historians and numerous politicians had vainly looked for in order to explain the whys and wherefores of famous decisions that were in contradiction with the declarations of the prominent figure who had made them, for instance, the Italo-German Alliance, signed by Ciano despite his detestation of the Nazis, and his acceptance of Italy's entrance into war against France and England without any attempt to resign his post when Mussolini announced it, although he disavowed it in his notebooks and in private conversations.

I discovered why Mussolini had launched into the Greek campaign and how Galeazzo Ciano had gone about convincing him to do so—because he too wanted "his war."

The reasons that led him to vote for the Grandi motion were finally explained to me, as well as the projects and the ambitions he cherished.

Had he really betrayed Mussolini? I believe that I can truly say that there was a moment when Galeazzo Ciano reached the decision that he could serve the national destiny better and perpetuate Fascism without Mussolini, but at the same time he never had the slightest intention of eliminating him in the true sense of the word.

The flight to Germany, which seemed so mysterious and so senseless to everyone at the time, was finally clarified to me, and

I was even given the opportunity to meet the man who, at the request of Edda Ciano, organized the first contacts with the Germans.

Some of the hitherto unrevealed aspects of social life under Fascism, the enigmas and origins of the Italo-German Alliance, as well as certain unsuspected personality traits of such men as Hitler, Goebbels, and Goering were illuminated for me by Edda Ciano and others.

The three months of terrible agony endured by Galeazzo Ciano behind the bars of his prison helped me to finally understand the martyrdom of a man and the suffering of his wife whose desperate battle to save her husband, carried on with heroic energy born of despair, had its equal in grandeur and dramatic intensity only in the death of her husband when all was lost.

That woman is Edda Mussolini Ciano, the oldest and favorite daughter of Il Duce and the wife of Count Galeazzo Ciano.

It was not easy to get her to retrace the past. I understood why she first drew back from her memories when we began to talk. I fully appreciated how unhappy it made her when she tried to force herself to relive certain episodes through memories and photos or treasured mementos extracted from crates she had never wanted to open again.

My first attempt to meet with her was completely unsuccessful. One of her lawyers sent a message saying: "Countess Ciano does not intend to receive a journalist or to recount her life story."

Several months later I had the opportunity of meeting her in Romagna, at the home of her mother, Donna Rachele Mussolini. I told her of my project. Edda Ciano said neither yes or no, but she did agree to receive me in Rome.

When I saw her again in Rome she told me that after the death of her husband she had realized that it was her duty to do anything possible to uphold her husband's reputation, but she wondered whether it was worthwhile to rescue him from oblivion by shaking the dust from those buried years.

In the interests of history?

"I do not believe in history," she told me. "I do not believe in it because I saw it being made before my very eyes and even participated in it. And I also know that it cannot be impartial. Its authors as well as its judges are human beings animated by passion, eaten up by ambition, rancor, or hate, who consider that

13

theirs is the sole truth. History can only be objective when enough time has elapsed for a proper perspective to develop. After a century has passed perhaps Mussolini, Ciano, and other famous persons from the Fascist era will be judged differently. But, for the moment, I believe that historical truth is an illusion, at least in their regard."

Material interest? That was out of the question.

"Even if I were dying of hunger, I would not recount the story of my own sufferings for money. Publishers have often asked me to write my memoirs and I have always refused, for the truth that lies hidden at the bottom of one's heart, a truth one secretly wishes to cry out to the world, cannot be simply tossed out to the public as food for gossip in exchange for some dozen millions of lira."

The need to rehabilitate her husband?

"I who knew him so intimately, so profoundly, also know that he has no need of that," answered Edda Ciano.

It was only after reading certain books about Mussolini and Ciano, as well as about herself, and disclosures made by people claiming to have known her well, people she had never laid eyes on, that Edda Ciano began to break through the icy reserve that she had imposed upon herself. Rage at such unfairness took over, and she agreed to answer my questions.

"I do not want you to write the 'life of Edda Ciano,'" she insisted. "I want our work together to give their true dimension to my husband and the others as well as to the historical events concerned. I do not care if, at the end of this book, the readers discover a Ciano greater or smaller, better or worse than the man they take him for today. I want the truth to be known. Whether he has been weak or whether he has been courageous is all the same to me, on condition that it be known to the full that he was not a traitor. That is something I know—and my father knew it too."

Edda Ciano could very easily have written this book herself, that is to say that technically speaking she could have taken pen in hand and covered blank pages with her memories. She did not do it because she feared that alone, in silent communion with her thoughts, she would have spared no one, would have struck out at people with her truth as one brings an ax down on an unsuspecting head. She wanted to avoid this, to spare those whom

14

she had already pardoned in her heart from a spate of vilification in which she might understandably indulge.

In agreeing to recall stages in her life and memories of events as well as of persons solely in relation to the questions I asked her, Edda Ciano provided a sort of refuge for herself. After several months of working with her I understood that she was answering everything without actually being forced to give herself away, to betray herself, so that her sense of decency, her modesty, remained intact.

On the other hand, she respected the rules of the game. She never evaded a ticklish question during our conversations. Even better, when her memory failed or when she was not sure about something, she would often accompany me to the home of certain witnesses and authorize them to tell me the story.

One of them, Zenone Benini, suffered several heart attacks after our visit, because of the emotion that overcame him when he recalled the last hours of Ciano that he had lived through himself. Despite her feelings and his, Edda Ciano conducted the interview with an obstinacy that amazed me, and I was astonished at this proof of her will to know everything, absolutely everything.

One of her friends, Tanino Pessina, described to me, in Countess Ciano's presence, how Galeazzo Ciano's notebooks were saved from the Germans during the course of their frantic searches for them in which the tragic mingled with the comic.

Also in the presence of Countess Ciano, Signor Tassinari, who had been one of the members of Mussolini's secretariat and had held the title of Prefect, revealed for the first time the plan of certain Fascists to save the five condemned men of Verona from death, as well as Il Duce's attitude toward them.

I discovered thus that Galeazzo Ciano had very nearly had his life saved twice—with the tacit accord of Mussolini. And then I understood the dilemma that Il Duce had faced and how much Ciano's death lay on his conscience. His compunction was such that after the death of Ciano he one day signed a photograph held out to him by an Italian woman with the phrase: "Mussolini deceased."

The subject of Count Ciano's female conquests came up in the course of certain conversations. Edda Ciano never avoided such discussions.

During these months of work the true personality—at least to my mind—of Edda Ciano was revealed to me. And this rendered her testimony even more intensely interesting.

I knew that Edda Ciano's character was exceptional, a mélange composed of temerity but also of reserve and timidity, of apparent toughness but equally of profound goodness and fidelity toward those she loved or had loved.

The tragedy of Galeazzo and Edda Ciano was extremely educational for me, a journalist likely to remain insensitive to and unmoved by the dramas that I come across because, and this is true of all my colleagues, professional rigor tends to overcome personal sentiments. But their story taught me to better understand human beings, to better appreciate the extreme limits of their nature, and helped me to discover and appraise the fragility of history, as well as the instability of human affairs.

II

SEVERAL MONTHS AGO IN PARIS, IN THE COURSE OF A FRENCH television program devoted to the Verona trial, I was asked if I held my father responsible for my husband's death. I replied that such a question was indecent, and I later learned that the public totally agreed with me.

Today, since you are asking me about my husband, I want to make my position on certain subjects quite clear from the start, with the idea of going into them more fully later on.

First of all, my refusal to answer the question when it was posed during the television broadcast was not due to any desire on my part to conceal the truth. I merely found it extremely disagreeable to be mercilessly exposed, by a camera revealing my innermost thoughts and deepest emotions, to millions of people unseen by me, enabling some of them to enjoy a morbid pleasure at the sight. But a book is something quite different, and so today I can say what I think about my father's role in the death of my husband.

Although he was not directly involved at the beginning, he did follow a policy of noninterference, either because of a lack of courage or that sort of fatalistic attitude that makes us say, when faced with a given situation, "Very well, so be it! The wheels have begun to turn, we shall see what comes of it all." Therefore, he was partially responsible for what happened.

It has been alleged that it was my father who ordered Galeazzo's arrest on the latter's return from Germany, where we had gone together after July 25, 1943, and that his trial and execution had also been carried out in conformance with my father's instructions.

That is not altogether true. My husband returned to Italy in October, 1943, having seen my father once the latter had been liberated from Gran Sasso by Otto Skorzeny's men. Galeazzo informed him of his desire to return to Italy and continue to fight, and my father did not oppose this. To be sure, there was nothing much he could have done, since we were in Germany and it was up to the Germans to oppose Galeazzo's desires or not as they saw fit. To be more precise, Mussolini did not formally agree but he did not arrest Ciano upon his arrival in Italy.

Then was Galeazzo's arrest decided upon by the Germans? I doubt this very much because apparently they did not wish to become mixed up in this affair. I believe that, with my father back in power, they were only concerned with getting Ciano off their hands and returned to Italy, so that the Italians could handle the problem themselves. This being said, they did hasten to communicate the date of his arrival in Verona to the Fascist police.

I am also certain that it was not my father who decided to hold the trial. He accepted the principle of it, because he could not do otherwise, thinking that he would be able to intervene in time to avoid any fatal ending to it. This is not only what he led me to understand when I saw him the day after my husband's arrest, but also what appears throughout the different statements and evidence that you have collected.

Besides, he considered the trial to be useless and politically inept, even harmful. The truly guilty had not been arrested, and the extremist elements among the Fascists were beginning to gain a considerable lead over the moderates and the realists in that particularly tense moment after the armistice of September 8, 1943, when Italy had already become divided into two camps.

As to the execution of the five condemned men at Verona, among them my husband, I believe that it was done without my father having been informed of the hour of execution, that the men who were at the bottom of this affair—whose leader was a friend of Galeazzo, Alessandro Pavolini, then Secretary of the Fascist Republican party—did everything possible to prevent the requests for pardon from reaching Mussolini and that he was not told of the execution until after the fact.

Would the Fascist extremists have reacted against a pardon or against a reprieve from the death penalty and the substitution of a jail sentence? Certainly they would have taken action, since they had made all the necessary preparations to kill the condemned men of Verona whatever the sentence handed down might be.

This is probably what my father wished to make me understand when he wrote me in one of his last letters: "You would perhaps judge me with more understanding if, one day, we could speak together looking into each other's eyes . . ."

He had also wished to impress this on one of my great friends, Father Pancino, a former army chaplain, when he received him shortly after Galeazzo's death and told him that the death had been motivated by "reasons of state." And not only did he not have the least word to say against my husband—on the contrary, he praised him several times—but one day he even cried, "They will pay me for that death! And above all, they had better not try to do to my daughter what they did to my son-in-law!"

Thus, at a certain moment, because of a mysterious conjunction

19

of circumstances, my husband's doom became inescapable, and I believe that he would have died whatever my father's attitude had been. Of course, I would have preferred that he be struck down by assassins, my father having no part in this dirty work, rather than by a firing squad, after the mockery of such a trial and such a sentence pronounced in my father's name.

The importance lies not in the *fact* of Galeazzo's death, but rather in the reasons for that death and the circumstances in which it occurred.

I am sure that at the relatively youthful age of forty my husband wanted to live—and who would not?—but I also know that he would have suffered less if his legitimate horror of death had not been augmented by despair and anger provoked by knowing that he was going to die for a crime he had not committed.

And that is why I have agreed to bear witness to these events.

I am animated neither by a desire for revenge against my father nor by the desire to make my husband into a hero or a martyr. I simply want my testimony to have its place in history along with that of others, since it cannot help but illuminate the real Galeazzo Ciano, one of the men whom I hold to have done so much for Italy, for Europe, and for peace. And this I insist upon, even though I was not always in agreement with him.

Why have I waited until 1974 to speak out? Perhaps because until now circumstances did not incite me to do so. Because I had always been asked to tell the story of my own life and I did not wish simply to provide food for gossip. This time you have asked me for a testimonial about Ciano and his epoch, and I accept the fact that in speaking of him I shall sometimes be compelled to speak of myself too.

Perhaps finally because if I had agreed to bear witness earlier, it would only have served to trample even more on the memory of Mussolini, and because a Galeazzo Ciano possessing other traits than those of a sensual pleasure seeker, a vain and inconsistent man, an ambitious, opportunistic, and Machiavellian politician, would not have been believable at that time. I wonder if even today I will be believed, since the witch hunt continues, and any political crime is automatically attributed to a Fascist origin, any bomb that explodes is assumed to have been set by a Fascist hand. The new generations do not even know what Fascism really was. And, in fact, who does know?

This is 1974, so you can imagine what would have been the lot of Edda Ciano's testimony in 1945 or 1960!

In those days the word of anyone in my family, including me, was doubted in relation to much less important subjects, such as financial questions.

For example, about 1959 I was at Monte Carlo and had occasion to chat with one of the Rothschilds, Maurice, as I recall, who is dead now. Our conversation had been the usual hodgepodge of social banalities, as is typical of such encounters, but suddenly Baron de Rothschild made some truly surprising remarks to me.

"I have learned," he said, "that you possess a painting belonging to my family that was taken by the Germans and eventually offered to you. It is a very rare Boldini, which we prized highly, and which represented a German or Austrian princess lying stretched out on a sofa."

And he continued to describe the painting in painstaking detail.

As I became increasingly astonished, and with reason, Baron de Rothschild went on. "I would not dream of holding you and your husband responsible for this theft, Countess Ciano. We belong to the same milieu and I do not want to sue you or cause a scandal. I am even prepared to buy back the painting from you so that it can be returned to the family. . . ."

I knew how many stories there were regarding artistic riches stolen by the leaders of the Reich, some true, some, on the other hand, invented out of whole cloth by people who wished to recover paintings they had actually sold.

Therefore, it was easy for someone to say that one of the German authorities had offered a stolen painting to my husband, especially since Goering had actually given a Boldini—*The Gypsy Dancer*—to Galeazzo, but in this case it was a picture that my husband had bought for himself.

Maurice de Rothschild may also have read my husband's notebooks and noticed a passage written on April 6, 1942: "When Goering came to Rome, we spoke of the possibility of bringing back to Italy certain works of Italian masters at present in France, particularly those paintings owned by Jews and sequestered by the Germans. Among the names he cited figured that of the Rothschilds, who owned several Boldinis. Today I received a gift of a Boldini from Goering and the letter he enclosed along with it began thus: 'Unhappily, there was nothing left at the Rothschilds . . .' "

And my husband had added: "If one day this letter should come to light, there is no doubt in my mind that people will say that I persuaded him to pillage the homes of Jews and that he lamented the fact that he had arrived too late."

Galeazzo's reasoning was unfortunately revealed to be exact, since Maurice de Rothschild was convinced that we Italians, having been placed in the same category as the Nazis at the hour of defeat, had been their associates in the field of pillaging.

I suppose that my obvious sincerity finally persuaded him that I was telling the truth, since he turned down my invitation to come and verify for himself that I did not possess the picture, and we discussed the matter no further.

The situation that arose with Maurice de Rothschild was relatively simple compared to the difficulty I had in convincing a partner of my husband's that I was right. This gentleman possessed 25 percent of the shares in *Il Telegrafo,* a Livorno newspaper, while Galeazzo had owned 75 percent of the stock.

The partner declared that he owned half of the stock in *Il Telegrafo,* and we were obliged to go to court to settle our differences. He was extremely taken aback when I exhibited my husband's will in which he had written, several hours before his death, that the newspaper shares he owned were to be divided between our children and myself and added: "Signor X. owns a quarter of the stock, I repeat, one-quarter of the paper . . ."

I remember asking the judges if they thought it possible that a man about to die would have lied about such practical matters. Finally the court settled the suit in my favor.

A third example is the never-ending battle that I had to contend with against a Jewish family from Livorno who had sold us their villa near that city when my husband was Minister of Foreign Affairs.

Not only had we paid for the villa, but we had even repaired and enlarged it.

Well, you will find this hard to believe, but that family found nothing better to do at the end of the war than to profit from the stories being bandied about concerning cases of pillaging by reclaiming the villa, no more, no less.

Despite the fact that I was able to furnish all the necessary documents, among others the bill of sale, established in due form with proof of payment, to demonstrate that we had bought it without the least prejudice to its owners, I was not only ordered to give back the villa but also to pay damages because, according to the judges who decided in favor of this family, the work that we had done on the house had affected the original conception as well as the beauty of the building.

This concludes my explanation of why I did not want to speak up earlier about more serious subjects. To be absolutely frank, since what the Cianos or the Mussolinis said regarding minor financial questions was not believed, I am skeptical even today about how much of what I have to say on all other matters will carry any weight.

That is one point. There are others that I would also like to clear up.

It has been written that Ciano became a Cabinet Minister solely because he was my husband—and that is false! My father appointed him to the Cabinet only because he knew him to be eminently capable of carrying out his duties as Minister. If that were not so, why did he not name my brothers, his own sons, to high positions in the regime?

Ciano has been described as passing himself off as my father's heir and proudly emulating him to such an extent that he aped Mussolini's mannerisms and way of speaking. This is true, but it was not because of any hidden design on Galeazzo's part. My husband seemed to mimic my father simply because he met with him several times a day for years and so unconsciously adopted certain of his characteristics. There are families, the Agnellis, for example, in which all the brothers and their friends speak in exactly the same way. Obviously they are not concerned with resembling each other.

Certainly it was Ciano's ambition to become head of state one day. Who does not dream of succeeding in life? And what other position could he have aspired to reach after such a career, since he was already Minister of Foreign Affairs?

However, though he felt himself capable of assuming such functions, he would never have thought of attaining the position by walking over the dead body—political or physical—of my father. As to that story of his being the "heir," in my opinion it was launched by those persons jealous of the fact that my father had great confidence in Ciano and consulted him about questions unrelated to foreign affairs and concerned with domestic policy, the party, or the conduct of military operations. And it is true that my husband's point of view often carried the day with my father, for example, in 1939 when Italy did not come into the war; in the campaigns of Albania and Greece that he advocated; in the—to be sure unwise—choice of a Secretary of the Fascist party; in the constitution of the next to the last government, which was called the Ciano Cabinet. The only area in which Galeazzo abstained from interfering was that of the army, because he knew that my father was jealous of those prerogatives; but he did excel particularly and showed qualities as great as those of my father in foreign affairs.

I can affirm that the cooperation between Mussolini and Ciano was absolutely complete until the removal of my husband, completely faithful on his part and completely confident on the part of my father.

It has also been said that Ciano was thrust from power because Mussolini knew that he had betrayed him. That is ridiculous. My husband lost his portfolio as Minister of Foreign Affairs solely because he was the victim of a secret plot hatched by Clara Petacci and her entourage—in which several Ministers figured—as a reprisal for two interventions of mine with my father; I had tried to convince him, documentary proof in hand, that his liaison with Clara Petacci was being publicized far too much and was harmful to his reputation and that her brother's fraudulent deals were bound to be just as injurious to his good name. As they could do nothing against me personally, they avenged themselves on Galeazzo by inventing a story of conspiracy and treason out of whole cloth. As I was not in Rome when this operation was carried out, I could do nothing to combat it. As you can see, it was not a political affair at all.

It is untrue that my husband betrayed my father by voting against him on July 24, 1943, during the last meeting of the Inner Council. Galeazzo Ciano voted for the Grandi resolution because he believed that it was in the best interests of Italy for the King to resume his responsibilities—especially in military matters—so that in a period of crisis, as was then the situation, the country would be unified in its own defense. But neither Ciano nor most of the other members of the Inner Council were thinking of deposing my father when they voted for the Grandi resolution. The coup d'etat traitorously carried out against my father was really engineered by men like Acquarone, Minister of the Court, the King and his General Staff, and Badoglio, who had Mussolini arrested. The vote of the Council served only to give the King a pretext and, in a certain sense, even interfered with the plans of the real plotters—who were on the General Staff or in the entourage of the royal palace—since a coup d'etat had been planned for several days later, August 4, in fact, and included the physical elimination of my father. Now I am not saying that some members of the Inner Council, among them Bastianini, Federzoni, Bottai, and Albini, were not thinking of removing my father from power. I am revealing these names because my father gave them to me himself when I saw him in Germany after his liberation from Gran Sasso. He added that of Grandi to the list, specifying that it was they and above all Grandi who were the real traitors and not my husband.

Another point—this regarding a matter that historians find mysterious—deals with the Cianos' flight to Germany on August 27, 1943, one month after the vote was taken at the Inner Council and the subsequent arrest of my father. No one could understand why Galeazzo Ciano had thrown himself to the wolves in taking refuge with Hitler and his cohorts, whom he had been openly criticizing for many months. The truth is that we had decided together to flee Rome and take refuge in Spain because we felt the vise closing on us ever more tightly, and my husband found it daily more difficult to face up to the new calumnies that were being published about his father, my father, and himself or to accept that a Fascist like Muti had been summarily executed.

We had little news about my family; I knew only that my father was alive, nothing more.

The few friends who had continued to visit us after the "kidnapping" of my father had soon ceased to call. The rare contacts that we had maintained with the royal palace had given way to a silence that became more menacing each day.

The only way to avoid arrest, or perhaps even liquidation, was to find refuge either abroad or on Vatican soil in Italy.

But the Holy See, where Galeazzo had represented our country until July 25, 1943, or so, refused to give us sanctuary. My husband was utterly crushed by this revelation that, though he had always been a true believer, the gates of the Vatican, those gates which had been open to so many people during the war, whether for humanitarian or for politically opportunistic reasons, were going to remain closed to him because he was Mussolini's son-in-law.

In order to leave the country we needed a passport as well as a visa. My husband's request for these documents remained unanswered by the government.

Therefore, we were forced to leave Italy clandestinely. This was complicated by the fact that we were not two but five—Galeazzo, our three children, and I.

My husband could have left for Spain alone, since the Spanish Ambassador to Rome, Fernandez Cuestas, had promised to see that he safely crossed the Italian and French frontiers into Spain, where General Franco's government had agreed to give him sanctuary. Unfortunately, such a journey, possible for a single person traveling alone, was impossible for five. And my husband absolutely refused to leave without me and the children.

As for me, like my brother Vittorio or other important personages in the regime, I could have placed myself under the protection of the German authorities in Rome if I had so wished, but Galeazzo stoutly refused to ask assistance from a regime that he had so often criticized!

The only solution remaining to us was to flee to Spain by air. However, we needed German assistance in order to have a plane placed at our disposal, and so we decided to ask the Germans for help. I myself undertook to establish contact with Himmler's representative in Rome—Dollmann—with a close friend, Admiral Bigliardi, as intermediary. After about ten days and two secret meetings with Dollmann I was informed that Berlin had agreed to give us a plane for our flight to Spain. The only reservation that had been formulated by Dollmann during our first meeting had concerned Galeazzo.

"You must be aware, Countess," he said, "that Count Ciano has not always been Germany's advocate. I do not know what the Führer will decide about *him*. While I am sure that there will certainly not be any problem concerning you."

"I see what you mean," I replied, "but in the present situation, the only person who could possibly explain what has really occurred during these last weeks is my husband. Therefore, if the Führer wants explanations, Count Ciano will give them to him."

Early during our flight we suddenly realized that we were not flying toward Spain. When we asked what was happening, we were told that it would be necessary to land at Munich for technical reasons and then we would continue on to Spain.

Once we were in Munich this "technical" stopover was transformed from hour to hour and day to day, first into a visit as "guests" of the Führer, then, after the armistice of September 8, into a visit as "virtual prisoners." We were to return to Italy only for Galeazzo to be imprisoned, then to die after a travesty of a trial, and for me to try to save him, fighting in vain against both the Germans and my father.

It is thus evident that Galeazzo Ciano did not voluntarily throw himself to the wolves by seeking refuge in Germany. On the contrary, he fell—and I along with him—into a deadly trap.

My last point concerns my husband's notebooks. Although their authenticity has not been denied, it has been said that they were altered in order to whitewash my husband. That is absolutely false. Neither he nor I altered or eliminated anything in those memoirs. I could easily have torn out a page or two that seemed embarrassing to him or to me, but I never did so, for that would have been contrary to my nature. I have always preferred to keep silent rather than to conceal the truth, and if I do speak out, I never beat about the bush.

My husband decided that the notebooks should be published because he wanted other countries to know what had occurred during the seven years that he had served as Italian Minister of Foreign Affairs, years that he considered a turning point in history for the entire world. He wrote the preface himself, in his cell at the prison in Verona, and he arranged for it to be delivered to me alone so that no doubt could exist as to the contents of the notebooks or his intentions. I was merely carrying out his instructions to the letter when I permitted the Americans to publish them, only after the death of my father and the end of the war in Europe.

I was also obeying his instructions when I accepted contacts with the Germans, and in particular with Frau Beetz, Himmler's special agent, to try to arrange for an exchange of the notebooks and other documents for the life of my husband. I must admit that at first I was shocked and disappointed when I received those instructions, believing them to be simply the response of a man whose head was at stake and who was willing to sacrifice his integrity to save it.

The extraordinary importance of the notebooks was apparent to the Germans. Himmler was the first to try to obtain possession of them for his personal use as an attack against Ribbentrop's political policy position. I then understood why Galeazzo, who could not tolerate the Führer's Minister of Foreign Affairs, had lent himself to such an operation, especially after he had been informed that Himmler had plans for negotiations with the Allies, plans that were put into concrete form soon afterward.

Consequently, it is plain to see that it was not only a desperate attempt by my husband to escape death that lent his notebooks their importance. As a matter of fact, I recall that Frau Beetz was put in contact with us while we were still in Germany at a time when there was no question of a trial. And even after the failure of the operation the Nazi authorities worked unceasingly to secure those documents. Also, after Galeazzo's death I myself was followed across all of Italy and even into Switzerland when it became known that they were in my hands. This is another proof that it was not only my husband's desperate attempt to escape death that made them so valuable.

Was it easy for me to pass over to the other side and find myself in the camp of my father's enemies? Since I had always loved and admired my father more than anyone else in the world, to such a point that I once promised him to be by his side if one day he should die in tragic circumstances, I was, of course, inconsolably heartbroken. But when I was forced by circumstances to throw in his face exactly what I thought of his attitude toward my husband, and when I wrote him harsh and angry letters, I was only speaking the truth as I saw it. My reaction would be the same if I were to find myself in the identical situation today, because it was the result of a turn of mind that had been inculcated in me by my father since my earliest childhood.

I suspect that the world knows and understands as little about my father, Benito Mussolini, as it does about my husband, Galeazzo Ciano, despite the fact that he seems to have been scalped and stripped, decorticated, so to speak, by everyone on earth, including the Americans who, after his death, took away a section of his brain to analyze it in their laboratories.

III

WHAT ALWAYS FASCINATED ME MOST ABOUT MY FATHER WAS his talent for never behaving like everyone else. The question of my parentage is a case in point.

Contrary to other children who have one mother and one father, or sometimes one mother and two fathers, I was said to be endowed with one father and two mothers. A veritable exploit!

A mysterious rumor had surfaced around the world according to which, although I was in fact the daughter of Benito Mussolini, I was not the daughter of Rachele Guidi, the mother of my younger brothers and my sister, but rather the fruit of a liaison between my father and a Russian woman of Jewish origin—Angelica Balabanoff. Those who spread this malicious gossip used as proof of its verity the fact that my birth certificate at the registry office in the Town Hall of Forli did not carry my mother's name and said only: "Edda, daughter of Benito Mussolini and of X . . ."

The real truth is quite different. My father did have among his female conquests a mistress named Angelica Balabanoff. I knew her when I was barely four years old and accompanied my father to the offices of his Socialist newspaper *L'Avanti* and then to those of *Popolo d'Italia,* after he had created it. I have retained a vague memory of a rather unattractive woman who would always run up to me and exclaim, "Oh, see how pretty little Edda is!" I disliked her and so would run and hide behind my father to elude her embrace.

But the idea that I am her daughter is pure invention, and the only reason that my mother's name was not mentioned on my birth certificate is that my father and mother were not legally married when I was born. They were good Socialist revolutionaries at that time and believed in what was called a "free union." According to Italian law in such circumstances, only the name of the father could be mentioned and not that of the mother, which explains the notation "daughter of X . . ."

My parents never accorded the slightest importance to this fable. My mother, Donna Rachele, would reply with a smile when someone spoke of it, "You know, they can say what they like, I don't really care, because when you give birth to a child it is you and no one else who feels the birth pains. And when Edda was born, it was *I* who felt those pains. If she is the daughter of Angelica Balabanoff, I don't see why I should have suffered as I did when she was born."

Knowing my mother as I do, I cannot believe that I would have been permitted to remain in the house for five minutes if I had really been the child of Angelica Balabanoff.

Later on, my father officially regularized his union with my mother, but, since we were in the midst of the First World War and also my father was bedridden in a military hospital with a viral hepatitis (if I remember correctly), he could not be present at his own civil marriage ceremony. One of his friends, a music professor, Maestro Limenta, stood in as proxy.

Although I was only five years old at the time, I attended the ceremony. For several weeks I was furious with Limenta because he had dared to marry my mother and thus become my second father, since I did not understand about a marriage by proxy.

Later I would joke about it, saying that I had not only two mothers but two fathers.

My father differed from others even in the way he raised me. When I was only several weeks old he found an ingenious way of making me fall asleep, ingenious but noisy. He would play the violin next to my cradle and would stop only when I was deep in sleep. But as soon as I no longer heard the music I would awaken and begin to howl. Papa would take up his instrument and the serenade would begin again—until the evening when he was obliged to light the candle and replay the violin sixty seven times! Then he became so angry that he had a fit and began to throw at my cradle anything he could get his hands on—pillows, newspapers, shoes. I owed my life only to the rapid and energetic intervention of my mother, who snatched me away from my crib into her protecting arms. I think that was the only time my father ever raised his hand against me.

Another time, irritated by my mania for twisting a lock of my hair while sucking my thumb before falling asleep, he purely and simply cut my hair short. I wept copious tears, so, to compensate for the loss, he attached an ear of corn with the silk hanging down from it above my crib, and that worked very well as it gave me something to wrap around my fingers.

He behaved in the same way with my mother. As he did not like long hair and dreamed of making her cut hers off, in order to convince her, he seized on the fact that bobbed hair was all the rage. But he had no luck with that, since my mother liked her long, ash-blond tresses, which in fact were very beautiful. Therefore, he decided to act. Seeing her pass by one day when he was sitting in the barber's chair, he called to her. She entered the shop and stood next to him. Under pretext of wanting to whisper in her ear, he made her bend her head down, and before she realized what was happening he had cut off her braids.

Later on I discovered another fascinating side to him. Unlike other fathers, one day he was at home with me, the next he would mysteriously disappear. My mother told me that he was traveling or in prison because he had wanted to stage a revolution and had fought with the police.

Contrary to other fathers, he had a shirt with only one sleeve, for fighting duels, and sometimes he would leave at dawn with gentlemen dressed very formally in black. He would often return to the house wounded but always bringing something home with him. One day he returned in the morning, carrying a little kitten in his arms and telling us that he had picked it up before the duel and had decided to keep it because it had brought him luck.

He often returned home with his clothes crumpled and creased, his derby hat battered and dented by the clubbings he had received from policemen. He would tell us all about his scuffles with them, miming the scenes and laughing heartily.

I recall that years later, after he came to power, a police officer requested an audience. Once inside my father's office the officer showed him an enormous truncheon and said in a quavering voice, "Your Excellency, would you do me the honor of accepting this gift? It is the club with which I often hit you at Forli during the demonstrations."

However, my father was not only a brawler, a rebel who became involved in riots. He was also a poet who knew how to create an enchanted world and how to give the most sparkling colors to the most lusterless objects. And above all, he never talked down to me.

During the First World War, when he left for the Front after enlisting, he wrote me many long letters as if I were an adult, never forgetting to enclose a little flower to show his affection. My mother read them to me because I was too young to know how to read, but I was very proud to have a father who realized that I was a big girl.

He kept a daily journal that he always carried on his person. This journal saved his life when a shell exploded at his feet and the book's binding stopped one of the pieces, which would otherwise have pierced his heart.

He gave me this diary upon his return. I kept it with me until 1944, when I lost it along with other important documents that I had left with a friend, a doctor at Ramiola. The Germans, who were searching for my husband's notebooks at the time, forced the good doctor to indicate to them where all the papers belonging to us were hidden, and he could not do otherwise than obey them.

When I grew older my father made me aware of the adult world as it really was, and this at an age when most children were still playing with toys.

I was perhaps the only little girl in the world to have learned the alphabet at the printing presses of a newspaper rather than at school on a blackboard.

In fact, my father did not want to send me to school and claimed that he was perfectly capable of teaching me what I should learn. He was quite right, moreover, since he had been a French professor for years.

As soon as I was old enough to understand things, he took me with him to his Socialist daily L'Avanti when he was going there to correct the proofs. I shall never forget the smell of ink that I inhaled at the printing press for so many years.

When my father was at the Front and I had to be entered at my neighborhood school, my mother sent him a letter informing him of this. He answered that he would soon be back to give me my lessons when he had finished giving the Germans theirs. Happily for me, my mother preferred not to wait, or I would have fallen far behind my comrades in reading and writing.

Thanks to my father, my evenings belonged to another world than that of most children. Not only did I accompany him to the paper but also to the theater or the opera—the famed La Scala, making use of the free tickets given to the newspaper.

Naturally, I didn't understand much of what was going on. But I looked extremely serious, didn't fall asleep, didn't fidget, showed no signs of impatience or boredom, and remained imperturbable even when the shouts and whistles of discontented spectators hurt my eardrums. One evening a spectator stuffed me with caramels during the entire spectacle because he was so excited at seeing such a young child so interested in the opera.

What pleased me more was the Galerie, the nerve center of Milan, where my father liked to stop after the show. The glittering lights in the gleaming chandeliers, all the appetizing morsels on the tables and the beautiful clothes fascinated me. I knew many other celebrated establishments, including Biffi, at the age of seven or eight. I was perhaps the youngest child in Italy to frequent such places.

During one of those evenings I saw a spectacle put on by the Excelsior ballet company. It was a revelation! For months afterward I danced on the tips of my toes, imagined myself dressed in a tutu and making graceful pirouettes on the stage. I dreamed constantly of becoming a ballet star, especially since I had strong, pretty legs and a good sense of rhythm.

But it would have been easier to ask my parents for the moon than to wrench from them the authorization to become a dancer. They were amused when I danced, but that was all. There was no question of even discussing it. A daughter who danced in public? Shameful!

In 1930 Papa created a scene with my fiancé because he had taken me to a nightclub. So you can see that back in 1920 he was certainly not ready to let me study the dance!

Though at that time they were convinced Socialists and revolutionaries, even bohemians, they still had the mentality of the petite bourgeoisie. I did not understand that at the time because I was only ten years old, but it did not take long for me to learn that my mother believed that a woman should remain a virgin until she married, have children, and spend her days taking care of the home. Papa had the same conception of woman's place in the scheme of things, along with an additional and typically Italian or Mediterranean concept—he felt that she should also be prepared to accept her husband's infidelities gracefully.

Therefore, the development of my artistic gifts was limited to the violin and then the piano. I still regret the dance, when I think of those childhood dreams of mine.

However, my father's old-fashioned views—antiquated when compared to the evolution that has occurred regarding woman's place in the world today, an evolution that I find questionable— did not prevent him from nourishing great ambitions for me. When I reached adolescence, he saw to it that I was first in many fields, not because of special favors but because he demanded that I be a perfectionist and give the best of myself.

I have often told the story of how he forced me to hold a frog in my hand to teach me to dominate my fear and repulsion without bursting into tears. And one day he made me cross the entire city of Milan in a carriage because the horse had shied, then bolted, and I was afraid to continue on.

I must admit that the control of my nerves he thus instilled in me served me well many times in difficult hours, and I think that I have had only one attack of nerves in my life—when I learned that my battle to save Galeazzo from death was lost. My father also inculcated in me several principles that later permitted me to weather each tempest I had to endure. A principle like the love of truth is, to my mind, completely prejudicial to those who put it into practice. But I have never succeeded in ridding myself of the habit of telling the truth, and at bottom I am glad of that.

He also emphasized the importance of love for one's country. I do not know exactly what that means, now that I have discovered all the evil things that can be done in its name, but I know that it still exists in me. For example, when I look at a snow-covered landscape, when I gather wild flowers or walk alone in the night, I like to imagine that the mysterious sky covered

37

with stars is only the roof of a great house called Italy and I wish, like my father, that all the inhabitants could be members of a united family.

I also learned to be responsible for my life and to accept the consequences of my acts without looking for excuses or an escape from my obligations, even when the malignity of the human race or the irony of fate turns the consequences into something quite different from those anticipated. He taught me never to be envious or mean, and I remember that in my childhood and after the last war I had a hundred occasions to suffer the consequences of such feelings in others. Finally, he instilled in me the awareness that man is born and dies alone.

The degree of osmosis between my father and me was such that to please him and obey him I learned how to do everything: I was the first Italian woman to drive a car and to wear trousers; I also learned to swim, to ride a bicycle, et cetera, at a time when women were not yet doing such things to any great extent.

But, despite his insistence on it, I was the only member of the family not to learn to fly a plane. And this is due to the fact that, when I was still a small child, my father had promised me that he would fly over the beach where we were playing and wave to me. At about the hour he was due to appear, a plane passed over our heads, signaling with its wings. Then, since he was flying too low, the pilot could not lift the nose of the plane and it crashed to the ground. When I heard that the pilot was dead, I was convinced that it was my father.

Fortunately for me it was not my father but a young man who had decided to hail his fiancée, who was also on the beach. However, the shock was so traumatic that I could never learn to fly, and to this day I am apprehensive when I must take a plane.

The cause of the drama that separated us lies in my love for my father. I had too much confidence in him to think it possible that he could ever make a mistake or not believe me.

Moreover, those same virtues that he had taught me helped me to judge my husband correctly and to understand that he had not betrayed my father but had only been misled into making an error of judgment. Certainly, it might be said that an error of such proportions can become criminal. But hadn't my father always said that love of country and love of truth should prevail over all other sentiments?

In that case, how does treason come into it when the future of the country is at stake?

IV

My mother, on the other hand, was the real dictator of the family, although her strong character was belied by her ingenuous exterior—delicate features, blue eyes, and blond hair. As far back as I can remember, she did only as she liked.

She was the sole member of her family to have wished to attend school. She walked seven kilometers in bare feet over a stony path full of potholes, carrying her only pair of shoes so as not to wear them out. Unfortunately, she was forced to stop school at the age of eight when her father died.

She went to work along with her mother and sisters in order to survive, rising at five in the morning and earning a few pennies a month. From then on, her only teachers were life and my father.

Her well-tempered character came into its own as the years passed. At only fourteen she was already defending Benito Mussolini, who had been her teacher at school when she was seven, against the sarcastic remarks of one of her employers, Chiedini; when he described with obvious satisfaction the agitator "Muslen's" (*Mussolini* in Romagna dialect) entanglements with the police and the beatings he received, she was the only one to stand up to him and declare her admiration for the man who was to become my father.

When she saw Mussolini again at seventeen, he began to court her assiduously. Since he was madly jealous, and she did not hesitate to defy him by dancing with other young men when she felt like it, when he stopped at Forli between his trips to Switzerland or elsewhere, my father sometimes shut her up in her room and served in her stead the clients of the inn (owned by his own father, Alessandro Mussolini) at which she worked with her mother. But even that did not prevent my mother from behaving as she wished.

When he proposed one day that she should live with him and bear his children—probably because he was tired of traveling ten kilometers daily to the Villa Carpena, where he had insisted that she live with one of her sisters to prevent her from going dancing and meeting other men—my mother answered yes immediately. Taking her bundle of clothes—which included a blouse, an apron, a dress and two handkerchiefs—and the seven or so pennies she had saved, she followed him.

When my father spoke of getting legally married, she obstinately refused to do so, even after my birth, saying that she preferred to be free to leave if one day she had had enough of life with him. It was only when an old mistress of my father's, Ida Dalser, began to call herself Signora Mussolini that my mother decided to marry my father in a civil ceremony, so as to cut the ground out from under the feet of any would-be "usurper."

If my father was the poetic, tolerant, and affectionate element in our education, the parent who understood our childhood dreams, my mother was the solid element, the one who had her feet firmly planted on the ground and assured the stability of the household, giving us many a clout to make us behave properly.

I remember that as a child I divided the world in which I lived into two parts: the prosaic, represented by my mother and my grandmother; the mysterious and adventurous, symbolized by my father. My father served as well as protection against my mother's slaps. If I had misbehaved, I would wait for him at the bottom of the stairs until his return home or hide under the bed and come out only when I heard his steps at the door, if her broomstick had not already dislodged me from my hiding place.

In 1916, when we were living in Milan, there was a frightful scene regarding a cock and a wooden cage. Unfortunately, my father was at the Front and not home to protect me against the thrashing my mother gave me. Still today I consider it to have been unjustified, and it made me reflect long and hard on the value of moral object-lessons.

My mother was expecting a child at the time, my brother Vittorio, and this too had profoundly disturbed me. I thought it the worst possible catastrophe, because I was convinced that the new baby would usurp my place in the family's heart. I must admit that even before Vittorio was born I had already made thousands of plans to get rid of the "intruder." And after his birth I put some of them into execution, without grave consequences, thank goodness.

To return to the cock. It was destined to become a restorative bouillon and give us a good feast with which to celebrate the birth of my brother (for everyone was certain that the baby would be male).

But while we awaited the event, the cock had to be fed. I was given the job of taking care of it and walked it each day so that it might eat en route and not cost too much for the family budget. I would take it into a field every afternoon so that it could stuff itself with slugs, seeds, etc., while I busied myself gathering chicory for our dinner.

Then we would return home, the cock walking ahead of me with an extremely dignified air, while I trotted behind, holding on to him by a string attached to one of his feet. The spectacle must have made passersby smile delightedly, as I must have given the impression of being dragged along by that imposing fowl, since I was very small and sometimes had difficulty in keeping up with him.

My problems began when my mother decided to make a cage for the cock. He had become quite imposing from all the rich food he had been eating outdoors, in fact so large that he was strong enough to escape from behind the metal bars my mother had placed in a corner of the kitchen to keep him enclosed. So my mother had decided on a cage that was to be closed on the top and on the sides. But it was difficult to find material with which to construct it, since we were at war and wood was so scarce that we had been obliged to fill our only stove with old rolled-up papers in order not to die of the cold. However, my mother would never have dreamed of renouncing something when faced with difficulties. On the contrary, she developed the theory that a handsome cage made of wood was absolutely necessary for the bird while he lived and that once he died the same wood would serve to heat the house. She had already discovered where she would be able to obtain the wooden planks.

The tenants of number 19 Via del Castel Morrone each had a box in the cellar into which they put different things such as wine, etc. And the covers of these boxes were made of wood. One of them was not in use at the time, because the tenant to whom it had been allocated had recently moved and the apartment was vacant.

My mother had decided to take several wooden planks from this box to make her cage. "Edda," she said to me one morning, "do me a favor. Go to the janitor and ask for the key to the cellar. But be careful, don't say why I want it!"

I was terrified of the janitor. He was a veritable ogre who reigned as dictator over the apartment building and its inhabitants. He had an enormous belly, always wore a beret slanting precariously on his head and kept a fat cigar stuck to one corner of his mouth. He opened the tenants' mail, shouted when he was not

43

content, and sang lustily off-key when he was happy. He was in a good humor when I knocked on his door and asked for the key, so that I was not only given the key but an affectionate tap on the head. But this euphoria was not to last very long.

When I came back fifteen minutes later to return the key, he asked, "What was your mother doing in the cellar?"

"She was only taking some wooden planks to make a cage for our cock," I replied.

I had spoken without thinking and found myself being shoved up the stairs, one of his hands holding me by the collar of my dress and the other giving me a slap on the behind.

I don't know what actually happened between my mother and the janitor because I immediately ran to my room and hid under the bed, in mortal fear of the storm that I knew was about to break over me. Once the cries had ceased and the janitor had departed I saw the broom handle passing to and fro under the bed; then my mother succeeded in dislodging me and I was soundly thrashed.

I realized that I should not have told the janitor that my mother had taken the planks, since she had told me not to mention them. But she had not told me what I should reply if he asked me; and, after all, I had only told the truth, which is what my parents had always taught me was one of the most important of moral virtues. So you can understand how bewildered I was at being beaten for telling the truth!

On another, more grave occasion my father was fortunately present in Milan and able to limit the damage when things took a truly bad turn.

Life was not very gay in our apartment on the Via del Castel Morrone; therefore, I spent most of my time outdoors in the courtyard of the building or in the neighboring empty lot.

Like all empty lots, it fascinated me. A railway line crossed it and trains had always attracted me as a lure to adventure in faraway places. Also, the lot represented an entire world of its own that had the faculty of changing its aspect depending on the season, the weather, or the time of day. Flowers grew there in the spring, and in winter we stumbled over dead animals. The children from the apartment building played in it during the day, and at night it served as a rendezvous for lovers.

One morning a group of gypsies set up camp in the empty lot. They were a revelation to me. Suddenly I was sick to death of my mother, whom I had to help with the housework, and of my maternal grandmother, who made me knit woolen scarves for the soldiers. My home seemed to me terribly sad and boring with its real bed, large windows, and unchanging stability when compared to the gypsies' home, which had wheels so that they could wander over all the roads in the world and stop wherever they liked on any old empty lot.

The gypsy children wore gold rings in their ears and beautiful multicolored dresses, while I had to content myself with my mother's discarded clothes that she had cut down and fixed for me. I didn't mind that the gypsy children were dirty—what child likes to be clean?—that they had lice in their hair or even that their parents were "wicked" people who kidnapped little girls belonging to other people, as my mother affirmed so as to frighten me away from them.

I had only one idea in my head—to leave, leave, go far away— and this despite the fact that our building, with its three enormous staircases and its large interior flagstone court, was an extraordinary universe peopled with all sorts of human beings, a milieu that I thoroughly enjoyed and of which to this day I retain a lovely memory.

I have already spoken of our peculiar janitor. But the tenants were more interesting. There was a murderer who had one day cut his wife to pieces, and a midwife who also did abortions. Across the landing lived a woman of easy virtue, who was always beautifully dressed, and next door to her an old count and his grandson, who lived in dire poverty but were always dignified and kept their distance from the rest of us. On the floor below us lived a girl who was a mystic and later entered a convent. Next to

45

her lived a well-preserved lady who indulged in table turning with the help of my father's foot, which constantly met hers when we held spiritualist séances. This good woman had a son and a twenty-year-old daughter whom my father decided to tutor in mathematics or English. These lessons ended when my mother discovered that they had the same aim as the spiritualist séances.

There was also a good, kind man who was extremely neurasthenic and passed his time balancing on the edge of his window ledge, saying that one day he would really jump, until the day when he found himself screaming with pain on the flagstones three flights down, most of his bones broken. Although the accident was horrible, it delighted his son, who was my age, and me. We profited from the general confusion it caused to play hooky from school that day, and while the wounded man was being carried away, begging to be finished off once and for all, we jumped up and down on a bed imitating his contortions on the ground.

Neither my mother's slaps nor the vows of love from the son of the spiritualist lady, my first flirt, deterred me from my project. "When I'm grown up, I shall marry you," the poor boy would declare. In the meantime, he gave me presents—balls of multicolored wool—that I accepted as my due, since he wanted to marry me. These gifts arrived through the air by way of a rope that we had installed between his balcony and mine. I accepted them graciously, but I continued to dream of leaving.

Each time that the possibility arose, I escaped from the house to rejoin my friends the gypsies, who became so used to seeing me among them that they began to consider me a member of the family. However, despite my pleas, they refused to promise to take me with them when they left.

"My mother says that you steal children, so why not steal me?" I would ask repeatedly.

"No!" they would answer. "You must remain with your own parents."

One day they announced that they were about to leave. I was in a panic. At home I became devilish, refusing to let my mother have a moment's peace and repeating incessantly, "I want to leave! I want to leave!"

My mother finally lost patience and shouted: "All right, if you want to go so much, then go. Go and don't come back!"

I was delighted because I could finally say to the gypsies, "You can take me with you now that my mother has thrown me out of the house." I ran to their camp, but they had left and in their place were only burning ashes, the sole trace of their stay.

I scoured the streets of the quarter to find them, but with no success. Then I sat down to weep, my chagrin growing by the minute. What was I going to do? Night was beginning to fall and everyone and everything looked bizarre in the light of the street lamps shining through the night mist. I shook with fear and began almost to regret leaving my home, where I would have been warm and safe. But I was stubborn and proud. Just as these two characteristics stood me in good stead against despair thirty years later when, in the general collapse of our fortunes, I no longer had anyone to whom I could turn, this time they helped me resist the temptation to turn back.

I was afraid, yes, but for all that, I did not intend to return home and face the raillery of my mother, who was likely to say, "Ah, there you are! So you've come back? But you wanted to leave us!"

Several people, thinking me lost, offered to help me, but I wanted nothing to do with them. To one of them, a lady I knew, I answered, "I'm waiting for the gypsies. My mother has thrown me out of the house and I don't want to go back."

Finally I caught sight of my grandmother, who had probably been informed of my whereabouts by the aforementioned lady. She came toward me and I forgot all my rancor and ran to hide my head in her skirts. How wonderful it felt to be protected!

At that moment immanent justice intervened. Probably to

demonstrate that she did not wish to scold me, my grandmother gave me some money and sent me to buy some pepper. I ran to get it, but on the way literally crashed into a baker who was leaving his shop with some bread. I fell to the ground, my brow split open, my face covered with blood. Immediately a group formed around me. My panic-stricken grandmother didn't know what to do; she thought I was going to die, especially since I was in a state of shock and remained totally silent, not even crying, because of the pain.

At last someone took charge—in every crowd there is always a thief, who steals, and a leader, unknown even to himself, who is revealed—so that my wound was quickly disinfected and I was taken first to my home, then to the doctor.

Papa had not yet returned home, and I only escaped a good beating—well merited this time—because of the terrifying aspect given my face by the blood and the mixture of Mercurochrome and other disinfectants.

Things became more complicated when we reached the doctor's. As soon as stitches were mentioned, my calm attitude abandoned me and I began to dash all over the room seeking escape. Papa, who had joined us in the meantime, did not do much to improve the situation because he was so upset.

As a result, I fought so wildly that I kicked the doctor in the chin and, in the process of trying to protect himself, he split my brow open a bit more. Instead of three stitches I had to have six, and it took the doctor longer to recover from the blows I had given him than it did me to recover from my injury.

Papa didn't even scold or lift his hand against me. I think that he understood how normal it was for an imaginative little girl like me to wish to live with gypsies.

Later on, when they had left infancy behind them, my brothers were no better treated than I, and it was not unusual to see them galloping down the stairways of the Villa Torlonia to escape from my mother, who would be running after them with her hand raised to strike. And they too would seek protection from my father when they were in trouble with my mother, who firmly believed that, Duce or no Duce, Benito Mussolini was a husband with the same duties as all other husbands, and that his children were like all other children and should not be treated any differently.

V

THOUGH IT MAY SEEM SLIGHTLY MALICIOUS, IT WOULD AMUSE me to demonstrate the truth of the following thesis: Benito Mussolini, my father, and Costanzo Ciano, my father-in-law, became famous thanks only to their wives—or rather to their desire to escape from their wives.

My father launched himself into political life so as to have an excuse to be absent from home a good deal of the time and thus be spared my mother's jealous scenes, to which he preferred the beatings of the police and his adversaries. As a result, he became Premier of Italy, Il Duce. My father-in-law, a naval officer by vocation and tradition, covered himself with glory in reckless military operations, preferring enemy cannon to the sharp reprimands and sour remarks of his wife. He became a Cabinet Minister, President of the National Assembly, and finally my father's official successor.

But both were considerate fathers, and their children loved them dearly, though Costanzo Ciano was more severe than Mussolini.

Galeazzo Ciano grew up under the tutelage of a father who applied the rigid principles of a naval officer and, like my mother, believed more in the persuasive force of a good thrashing than in the virtue of a moral lesson. He succeeded in inculcating the Christian faith in his son, along with a deep sense of family love and trust as well as the importance of duty and love of one's country. He also kept him away, or tried to do so, from the usual female encounters enjoyed by boys of his age.

For example, in order to prevent Galeazzo from "knowing women," Costanzo Ciano insisted that his son attend preparatory school in Livorno dressed, despite his fifteen years, in a sailor suit cut down from one of his father's discarded uniforms, and in a kind of sailor beret instead of the usual straw hat worn by his comrades. When asked one day by Tito Torelli, a friend of his son's, why he disguised Galeazzo in such a fashion, Costanzo Ciano replied, "Because I want him to find it impossible to accompany you and the others to the whorehouse."

Whenever Galeazzo did a favor for a friend while he was a Cabinet Minister, certain of his detractors held that he only did so in order to publicize his power and to show those indebted to him how useful he could be. They implied, in other words, that a favor from Galeazzo was not a gesture of friendship but rather of condescension.

In response I will let Tito Torelli, his childhood friend, who never engaged actively in politics, speak:

"When he was a student in school at Livorno, Galeazzo more than once accepted, without turning a hair, punishment for having copied from his comrades when, in reality, it was he who had given his homework to them so that they might copy it, because he was superior to all of us in most subjects. He could have defended himself by revealing that it was they who had copied his work, but he never did so because that would have been contrary to the principles of benevolence, instilled in him by his mother, and of honor, taught him by his father. The latter would have given him a good kick in the behind if he had learned that his son had tattled on his comrades."

Many years later, when he knew that he was condemned to death, my husband had the same attitude toward his companions in prison. He continually protected them from the vindictiveness of his own enemies, reassured them when he could and even, when the occasion arose, took care of an ill prisoner, jokingly remarking —with his usual sense of humor—that the man would later be able to boast that he had been nursed by a Minister of Foreign Affairs. This story originated with Zenone Benini, a Cabinet Minister in the Fascist regime who had been imprisoned at Verona for having served as a liaison agent between the regime and the Inner Council.

Although Galeazzo Ciano was a good comrade and an intelligent, even brilliant student, excelling in Greek and Latin, this does not mean that he was completely virtuous or in the least exemplary at school in Livorno. He lost his temper easily and was, I believe, at one time expelled from school for having thrown an inkwell in the face of a professor who had infuriated him.

Galeazzo was deeply affected by the First World War. Like many of his comrades, he regretted that he was too young to enlist and fight against Italy's enemies.

When my father created the Fascist party he very soon had a choice recruit, Costanzo Ciano, who placed at Mussolini's service his fame and his Gold Medal, the supreme national decoration, a distinction that he had won during the First World War fighting in the Adriatic against the Austrians.

But curiously enough Costanzo Ciano, who had plunged headlong into political life, did not wish his son to become involved in politics. He even forbade Galeazzo's friends to take him to a Fascist cell meeting, shouting, "I'll beat the devil out of you if I catch you taking my son there!"

But his interdiction was unsuccessful. Galeazzo Ciano, who was studying law and political science at the University in Rome, took part in the March on Rome and played an active role in the demonstrations. He was nineteen years old.

Descended from a family of admirals and ship owners, Galeazzo inherited from his parents and grandparents a strong will and great ambition. He might have become an admiral, but he preferred to enter the field of journalism. He even dreamed of becoming a man of letters.

While still at the University my future husband was also a reporter for a Fascist newspaper, *L'Impero;* then later he became its theater critic. He even wrote two plays—*La Demenza di Hamlet* and *Il Fondo Oro.* The latter, played by a celebrated actor, Petrolini, was very successful, and the achievement helped to raise a self-esteem that had fallen low indeed from the boos with which *La Demenza* had been greeted. My ·mother-in-law, who had traveled from Livorno to Rome to see it, told me, thirty years later, that she could still hear the boos and whistles of the audience and had never felt so ashamed as at that spectacle.

Galeazzo's artistic career never went any further. But Rome's literary milieu had opened its doors to him. He was twenty years old, charming and aristocratic. He made many female conquests, one of whom was the celebrated actress Paola Borboni.

However, Costanzo Ciano put a stop to this gay and frivolous life, and Galeazzo was ordered to turn to more serious occupations. He chose the diplomatic corps and at twenty-two passed the competitive examination to become Secretary of Embassy, at the same time as Filippo Anfuso, a friend whom he saw much of as the years went by and who became his principal private secretary when Galeazzo was named Minister of Foreign Affairs. The first to answer "present" in 1943 when my father was liberated by Skorzeny and reconstituted a government, Anfuso then became Undersecretary of State in the Social Republic of Italy.

Galeazzo was appointed to Brazil, where he remained for one year before being transferred to Argentina. After that he was sent to China, then returned to Italy, where he was appointed Italian Ambassador to the Holy See.

That was when we met. He was twenty-seven and I not yet twenty; the year was 1930. I had spent a year in a finishing school for young girls of good family in Florence and was now taking private courses. I had a good sense of humor and a vivid imagination, but was extremely timid. I wanted to live life to the hilt, but was completely unsophisticated as I dreamed of love and adventure. And I adored my celebrated father.

Galeazzo had tasted most of life's pleasures and was a man-about-town who attended all the most fashionable social functions. He was ambitious and well aware of what would help him to succeed in having a brilliant diplomatic career.

Many stories have been told about how we first met. One version had it that our parents organized our encounter during a theater party. According to another version, favored by certain historians, Il Duce, having learned that his daughter wished to marry Galeazzo Ciano, was surprised because he did not know that Costanzo Ciano had a son. He hastily had the young man investigated, the report was favorable, and so he immediately gave him a job that would be commensurate with his status as the son-in-law of Il Duce. Further accounts described Galeazzo Ciano as happy with such a lucky windfall and learning foreign languages to please his father-in-law, flying a plane only so as not to displease his tyrant of a wife, spending his days repeating "yes" to Il Duce and having only a single word to say when at home—"Amen."

All those tales are 100 percent false. Apropos of our first encounter, for example, no one arranged it and our parents had absolutely nothing to do with it. I knew Maria Ciano, Galeazzo's sister, whom I liked enormously and saw constantly at the parties we both attended at the homes of mutual friends. I had never met her brother, Galeazzo, because, having entered the foreign service several years earlier, he was always abroad. Maria had shown me his photo and I had found him very handsome—that was all.

One evening, at a ball given in Galeazzo's honor since he had just returned to Rome, Maria introduced me to her brother. We danced together all evening and when we left each other we promised to meet again very soon. That encounter occurred on January 27, 1930, and was destined to put an end to a very restless and troubled period in my sentimental life, much to the relief of my worried parents.

Ten days earlier I had broken my engagement to a young man I did not love and whom my family had wished me to marry. And when Galeazzo and I met I was preparing to run away to Yugoslavia with a friend so as not to be forced once again to marry a man against my will.

I have no idea how that escapade with Federico—Kiko—my "vacation flirt" would have ended. To tell the truth I never thought about it, but regarded it as a Jules Verne adventure that would permit me to unite the useful with the agreeable, that is to say help me avoid having a husband imposed upon me while at the same time enjoying a handsome voyage. Now, forty-four years later, I cannot imagine what my father would have done if that expedition had really taken place!

Why did I wish to run away when I was not yet twenty? Because I had been battling for an entire year against my parents, who had decided that I must marry. They were influenced in this decision by my paternal aunt, Edwige, as well as by the number of my flirtations, which were beginning to annoy them.

My first flirtation occurred in 1929 during a cruise I made to India. An article appeared in the gossip column of a foreign newspaper declaring that Mussolini's daughter had an Indian boyfriend. Fortunately, the truth was quickly revealed—that the "flirt" was simply a young Indian of prominent family who had served as a guide, taking me to visit some temples as a gesture of courtesy toward Benito Mussolini, who was famous in India for his ideas and because of his friendly relations with Mahatma Gandhi, who had visited us at the Villa Torlonia.

I remember that as the ship carrying me back from India entered the Gulf of Naples I sensed that catastrophe was nearing. Very shortly afterward I discovered that my forebodings had been well founded. As soon as I arrived in Rome, my father told me of his keen desire to have me meet "a charming young man whom you will certainly find attractive . . ."

I understood immediately that my parents wanted to marry me off as soon as possible. A priori, I wasn't really against the idea. Also, when I was a young girl, we were not in the habit of disputing the orders or desires of our parents. Papa wished me to take a husband, and I could only bow my head and obey.

What did irritate me was the family's maneuvers to convince me. After conversations with my mother and my paternal uncle Arnaldo, and after I had seen the fine hand of my aunt Edwige at work, the entire affair began to resemble an unattractive plot.

Aunt Edwige's favorite hobby was to arrange marriages for the spinsters of the family and to discover that the Mussolinis had noble origins. We all smiled when she established our family tree and had our coat of arms—found goodness knows where—placed above the main entrance of our house in Romagna, Rocca delle Caminate. She had made a fine match for her own daughter, whose husband was young, intelligent, and of noble lineage. He too came to a frightful end during the events of 1945 when his cadaver was dragged through the streets.

When I discovered that it was she who had first decided to marry me off without asking my opinion or giving me the possibility of choosing my husband, I became extremely irritated. However, there was nothing I could do about it, especially given Aunt Edwige's personality. When I was still a child an icy chill would come over me whenever her imposing silhouette appeared at the door of our apartment in Milan. She would invariably say to me in a peremptory tone of voice, "Edda, take my valise and put it in my room." And I would drag the suitcase painfully to her room, even though it weighed twice as much as I did.

I knew that I could not object or call on my father for help. He had enough trouble trying to arbitrate the conflicts which constantly broke out between my aunt and my mother over questions of precedence and power. These struggles between the two women went so far that when his sister dedicated a school, my father would make haste to draft his wife to dedicate a hospital, or vice versa, in order to have peace at home. So you can see that Papa would not have risked starting a quarrel in the family—and, besides, he himself found the young man perfectly suitable as a prospective son-in-law.

Pier-Francesco Mangelli was the son of industrialists from Forli in Romagna. He was of noble family, rich, handsome, and twenty-seven years old—the proper age, according to Aunt Edwige, for the husband of a young lady of nineteen like myself.

I was, as I have said, perfectly willing to marry, but I wanted to know more about my fiancé. Therefore, I telephoned his younger brother and invited him to tea. When he arrived I was agreeably surprised by his attractive face and manner.

I asked questions regarding Pier-Francesco's sleeping attire, whether he smoked, drank, liked sports. Astonished by the queer turn of the conversation, he tried to answer as best he could. It turned out that my fiancé wore pajamas, did not drink, smoked very little, and liked sports. Although the portrait was not the sort to fill one with enthusiasm, I could see indications of some positive aspects. The fact that he wore pajamas rather than a nightshirt, and was athletic, was certainly a plus. I told myself that with time, if he were intelligent and an agreeable companion, I could perhaps fall in love with him.

But my enthusiasm quickly cooled when I asked what his tastes were in the realm of sports. The younger brother informed me that he had to precede his brother into the water so as to be able to tell him if his dive had been up to snuff and if not what errors had occurred.

I decided then and there that Pier-Francesco must be slightly priggish and finicky—not at all my cup of tea. But I didn't see how I was going to solve the problem. I did like his younger brother, who was handsome, amiable, and even amusing. But he had one drawback against which neither he nor I could do a thing—he was the younger son and could not take precedence over his older brother.

So I was forced to accept my aunt Edwige's second step in the "marriage operation" and meet my destined fiancé. I must admit that my parents as well as those of Pier-Francesco arranged things very well indeed. The surroundings of the Villa d'Este at Stresa were propitious to romance. Also, Pier-Francesco's father, mother, brother, and sister were charming. He and I almost glared at one another, as though saying, "You know that I had nothing to do with this, the others forced me." Since he was not at all stupid, he saw right away that I was not attracted to him. And I was relieved to see that I was not particularly his type either.

Fortunately Pier-Francesco was often abroad, continuing his studies, and so I was able to choose a new boyfriend and have two strings to my bow. He was a young Jew whom I met at the home of friends. Everything was fine until the day I wrote my father that I wished to marry my new friend. Papa had already been informed of our liaison, in any case, because I was escorted everywhere by a Secret Service man.

I was immediately deluged with my mother's violent remonstrances; my uncle Arnaldo went to see the young man's family to inform them that their son could not possibly dream of marrying Mussolini's daughter, whereupon, being Orthodox Jews, they declared that they were also opposed to such a marriage. Then my father confiscated my beautiful automobile—a measure that proved by far the most efficacious.

After the rupture with my Jewish boyfriend, of whom I had been very fond, Pier-Francesco Mangelli and I went to Spain, accompanied by the family as chaperons, in order to become better acquainted with each other. We became officially engaged after our return from Spain, and things would have followed their normal course if my fiancé had not made an enormous blunder with my father.

In early January of 1930, after a stay of several weeks in Liège, he wrote to Papa asking for an audience. He came to Rome and saw Papa in his office at the Villa Torlonia. When they sat down to dinner, after their conversation, Pier-Francesco's sheepish manner betrayed the fact that something unpleasant had occurred.

During the entire dinner, he could barely swallow a mouthful and visibly suffered a thousand torments. When I discovered that he had asked my father how much of a dowry he could expect, and that Papa had sharply replied that his own wife had brought him no dowry and therefore his daughter had no need to do so, I felt sorry for Pier-Francesco. But I did think that he had really lacked any sense of tact or psychology in bringing up monetary questions so unnecessarily and so bluntly, since my father was, after all, Il Duce.

Two days after that memorable evening Pier-Francesco was still in Rome, trying anew to be received by Papa. He wanted to explain to him that he regretted having expressed himself so badly, that he had not meant to say what he had, et cetera. But my father refused to acknowledge his existence, and if he had continued to hang about the Villa Torlonia, I believe that the police would have been ordered to arrest him. On January 17, 1930, I was told to write a note to Pier-Francesco notifying him that our engagement was annulled.

So there I was, free again and rather happy. Ten days later, on January 27, I met Galeazzo.

But in the ten days between those two dates, in order to forestall any other matrimonial surprises that might be dreamed up by the family, I had instructed my friend Federico to organize the expedition to Yugoslavia that I have previously mentioned. That enterprise was cast aside with the appearance of Galeazzo, thanks to the complicity of his sister Maria, who was a great help in encouraging and facilitating the rendezvous that led to our marriage.

VI

ONE AFTERNOON GALEAZZO AND I WENT TO THE MOVIES TO see an American film on Polynesia called *White Shadows*. As usual, the security guard followed hot on my heels.

Perhaps the beauty of the images on the screen had put Galeazzo in a romantic mood because he murmured in my ear: "You must know, Edda, that I'm in love with you. Will you marry me?"

"Why not?" I replied, and was thereby engaged to a man whom I loved without the intervention of my aunt Edwige or machinations by other members of the family. Pier-Francesco and other predecessors were all forgotten.

When I returned to the house that evening I ran to my father's room, where he was changing clothes to attend a reception. I thought it prudent to have his blessing before announcing the news to my mother. My father had always been my confidant, just as I was the person in whom he confided the most. So it was natural that he be the first person to whom I spoke of my choice.

"Papa," I said precipitously, "I became engaged this evening to Galeazzo Ciano, the son of Costanzo."

My father was in the process of putting on his trousers. He stared at me incredulously for several seconds, then dashed through the house, holding his trousers in his hand and shouting, "Rachele, Rachele. Edda is engaged! This time it's true! And I certainly approve of the young man!"

He was no longer the statesman, the "great man" of his time whom the world either admired or feared. He was a father who had just learned some marvelous news—that his daughter, for whom he had always nourished the highest ambition, was happy and was sharing her happiness with him.

My mother too was delighted. But my brothers were skeptical because they believed that I was merely sowing my wild oats once again and that I would never really settle down. It is true that my mother would probably have preferred to see me marry Pier-Francesco Mangelli, because he was from a respectable land-owning family in Romagna, where she grew up. But Galeazzo's family, though not from Romagna, was extremely honorable, and Costanzo, his father, had given my family proof of his faithful attachment. Therefore, the Mussolinis were prepared to welcome him with open arms.

Even to this day, however, I do wonder if Galeazzo's lineage did not have something to do with the severity of my mother's judgment of him after July 24, 1943.

Two weeks later, on February 15, 1930, Galeazzo came to the Villa Torlonia to ask officially for my hand. This time my parents did not need a visit to Spain, a meeting in Stresa, or the confiscation of my automobile to oblige me to accept a fiancé. Everyone was overjoyed.

My father, despite being the powerful Il Duce, felt awkward and ill at ease at the prospect of receiving a young man who was going to ask him for his daughter's hand. Therefore, a little stage managing was in order: my father was to receive Galeazzo in his office, while my mother and I waited in a small salon on the same floor for my father to confirm my engagement officially.

Galeazzo arrived at three o'clock, dressed in a conservative gray suit, gloves in hand, as befitted a young man coming to ask for the hand of a well-brought-up young lady. I did not see him enter the villa, but he told me later that he had been very nervous and almost stumbled as he walked up the path.

We were all extremely nervous. It may seem stupid that I should have felt so emotional since I knew what the outcome would be. But that proceeding was to seal my choice and constituted a turning point in my life as well as in that of my parents. While we were merely discussing projects—in the air, so to speak —everything had seemed very simple, but now I was going to leave the family circle, to create my own family, and that was another story. I understood that my decision was going to lead to an irreversible change in my life.

When Galeazzo entered his office, Papa—according to what my fiancé told me after the encounter—plunged his nose into his papers as though he were absorbed in studying a very important document. Then, at the end of several seconds, having gathered his wits together, he raised his eyes and pretended to discover by chance that Galeazzo was there.

I have never known exactly what they said to each other. But after several minutes my father called to me and my mother. When we entered the office, he and Galeazzo greeted us with wide smiles, and I noted that they both seemed relieved. As soon as my father had told me that Galeazzo had asked for my hand and that he had granted it, my fiancé took out of his pocket a small jewel case, which he opened. He then took from it a ring and placed it on my finger to seal the engagement.

Everybody embraced, and we were finally permitted to leave. Once on the staircase we finally exchanged our first real kiss. Silly though it may sound, I knew from the moment of our first encounter that with Galeazzo everything would be beautiful, clean, and pure, because we were both serious about each other.

My mother almost spoiled the romantic and touching side of all this when, pushed by goodness knows what demon, she insisted upon describing me to Galeazzo, after having embraced him, in the following terms: "You know, Edda doesn't know how to do anything. She can't sew, cook even an egg, run a household. As to her character, I won't even speak of that. But I'm her mother, and I wanted to warn you."

Though flabbergasted by this outburst, Galeazzo managed to smile, but I am sure that in his innermost heart he must have wondered if he were not entering a truly eccentric family. And I readily admit that my family's mode of life must have confirmed this impression during the thirteen years of our life together.

Galeazzo even had to suffer my father's remonstrances for having dared to take me to a nightclub while we were engaged. My father regarded such places as beyond the pale. La Bonbonnière, as I believe it was called, was in truth very chic and frequented by the best and most respectable people. It was more like a salon, where one could have a drink and dance, than like a night spot with a show, where the darkness and an ambiguous ambiance might perhaps corrupt the morality of a young lady of good family.

But my father, who was not particularly prudish, and who indeed never hesitated to enter into an amorous adventure just as long as the woman was curvaceous and attractive, kept to certain principles of his own; anything that touched on the artistic world was obviously corrupt, so that cabarets, nightclubs, and other places of amusement were, to his mind, simply the antechambers of whorehouses. Therefore, even though the reports given him by those confounded security guards, who still constantly dogged my steps, did not record anything wrong that might have harmed my reputation, my father still gave my fiancé a good scolding.

· Realizing that he could never persuade my father to change his attitude, Galeazzo intelligently chose to keep silent and let the storm pass. For not only did he love me too much to let such an unimportant incident become a bone of contention, but also he was aware that his future father-in-law, who was lecturing him on the necessity for moral standards, was his Duce and his Premier. I imagine that his dressing-down by my father on that occasion was Galeazzo's first indication of how difficult it was to be the son-in-law of a head of government of my father's stature.

Finally the great day arrived. On April 24, 1930, I married Galeazzo Ciano.

Like all weddings, mine took place amidst enormous confusion. My brothers profited from the general disorder by being able to avoid going to school for several days. My mother swore that she would not be duped another time and that the next wedding would take place at a hotel—a promise that she kept, moreover.

She did not let anyone help her with organizing the reception at the Villa Torlonia. This was not a small affair because we had to place some four hundred people in the gardens, taking into account all the protocol problems that entailed plus dealing tactfully with the susceptibilities of some of the guests, et cetera. Then, the preparations concerning the family were exhausting physically as well as mentally. I myself had to have many fittings because, for the first time in my life, I had a dress—my wedding dress—and a trousseau designed by a top couturier.

Finally the presents had to be placed in the drawing rooms and exposed in such a fashion that no one would be vexed. There were an impressive number of gifts that flowed in from all over the world, some superb, some modest and sometimes very touching. There would have been even more if my father had not requested that they be addressed to charity organizations whenever possible. The King and Queen of Italy offered me a beautiful brooch worth a small fortune. I used it fourteen years later to pay those who helped my children pass the border into Switzerland when bad times fell on us.

But it was my father who gave me the greatest surprise. His offering was a great, magnificent lace tablecloth, and the fact that he had thought of such an original, beautiful, yet useful gift gave me extraordinary pleasure.

I was neither made up—at twenty I hardly needed to be—nor coiffed in any way differently from other days, but my shoes were new and too narrow. Tired, my feet hurting, I had only one thought—that the day finish quickly.

At eleven in the morning we went to San Giuseppe, the church on the Via Nomentana, where both the civil and the religious ceremonies were celebrated, in conformity with the Lateran accords that had been signed by my father and Pope Pius XI. Immediately after the ceremony we went in procession to Saint Peter's, with Papa in the lead, Carolina Ciano on his arm.

There was no official ceremony. We simply went to the cathedral to kiss the foot of the statue of Saint Peter, a custom followed by most of the young brides and bridegrooms of the time, as well as their guests. Papa was the only one not to respect this custom.

We returned to the Villa Torlonia for the wedding feast at about three in the afternoon. The distribution of sweetmeats, photo sittings, and finally the reception followed.

Many years later I read in a book that at the end of that day, once the last guest had left, Mussolini and his children played ball amidst the remains of the reception, hindering the servants who were trying to put things in order. I cannot understand how people can wish to write such unbelievable tales when the truth is so much more amusing than their lies. Those who wanted something sensational to write about needed only to assist at my departure on my honeymoon to gather picturesque material for a story.

In the early evening hours I changed my clothes and sat at the wheel of my beautiful Alfa-Romeo with Galeazzo beside me. This in itself was rather unusual, since it was usually the husband who "took" his wife on their honeymoon. We drove off toward Naples, and my father, who had had some difficulty keeping his emotions in check during the day, could no longer control himself when he saw us leave. So he immediately jumped into his car and, my mother by his side, began to follow us. Of course they were not alone, because several police escorts had time to take to their cars and accompany him.

I don't know how long they might have followed us—perhaps as far as Naples, where we were to embark for Capri—but after over twenty kilometers, when I saw my father's car behind us, lost in the cloud of dust we were making (at that time we did not yet have handsome asphalted roads), I stopped.

"Where do you want to go, Papa?" I asked him. "It's ridiculous of you to follow us like this."

"I just wanted to accompany you some of the way," he replied sadly.

"Do you think that's wise? You and Mama are swallowing gallons of dust. In any case, we must leave each other. Please return home and stop worrying. Galeazzo and I will call you as soon as we arrive in Capri, I promise."

My father remained silent, knowing that of course he must turn around and go home. He was discovering, for the first time really, that his "little princess" was lost to him forever. My mother kissed me and at the same time slipped a thousand-lire note into my hand, whispering, "This is so that you can buy yourself anything you need."

Galeazzo, who had seen it all, smiled incredulously. He understood that a father might wish to prolong his farewells with a departing daughter—he had done the same with his parents— but he could not understand the fact that his mother-in-law imagined he might not be able to provide for his young wife's needs.

Galeazzo had not finished with surprises that day.

We received a triumphant welcome from the population of Capri. Amid the fanfare and flags, I was red with shame and shyness, wishing I could hide away from all the prying eyes. I would not have been embarrassed under other circumstances. But the idea that all those people, who knew full well what was going to occur later, were looking at me as though I were the sacrificial lamb, was too much for me.

And then my beautiful young girl's dreams about being carried off by a Prince Charming were dissipated as soon as I was alone with my husband in our suite. I was so paralyzed at dinner that I could barely swallow a morsel, but I continued to order dishes in order to keep the maître d'hotel with us a bit longer. After dinner I ran to barricade myself in the bathroom.

"If you come near me, I shall jump into the sea from the top of Faraglioni!" I shouted to Galeazzo, pointing to the enormous rock visible outside the window, as I dashed from the room.

Galeazzo didn't make a fuss or lose his temper. Not only did he give me supplementary proof of his sense of humor and his tact, but he allowed me to discover another aspect of his personality of which I had been unaware until then—his art of persuasion.

"I know that you are capable of doing what you say," he replied through the bathroom door. "I wouldn't dream of preventing you from doing whatever you wish. But just explain one thing to me. How will you climb to the top of the rock so as to leap into the sea?"

His reasoning was so logical that I opened the door, looked again at the rock, then turned and met his smile. We both exploded with laughter. My panic was overcome. I was delighted!

VII

WHEN MY HUSBAND AND I LEFT FOR CHINA, SEVERAL MONTHS
after our marriage, his parents and my mother accompanied us
to Brindisi and stayed to wave good-bye as the ship left the harbor.

Galeazzo was amazed when I took his arm and said, "Very
well, that's enough now. Shall we go and eat?" He couldn't believe that I was so unemotional about leaving my family for such
a long absence on the other side of the world.

I must say that he should have noticed long before that I was
not very expansive about revealing my innermost feelings. Once
we had decided to become engaged I merely wrote him a short
note informing him that all had gone well at my house and asking
him briefly how his parents had reacted to the news. After our
engagement had been officially settled with my father and Galeazzo
had offered me my engagement ring I sent him a ring in turn,

offered in an envelope delivered by a security guard. This brought me an ironic letter from him which said in substance: "I knew that I could expect anything of you, but you will never fail to surprise me. Your sending me a ring by way of a policeman does not lack originality."

I always believed that as the years went by Galeazzo would become accustomed to the Mussolini turn of mind. But I don't think he ever really did.

On the day in March, 1941, that my hospital ship, the *Po*, on which I was working as a nurse, was sunk in Albania, my father and my husband were making an inspection trip in the area. Thus, Galeazzo was able to follow closely my father's reaction when the sinking was announced. Once my father had learned that I was safe and sound he simply telephoned to my mother and said, "Edda has been in a shipwreck, but she is unharmed. I'll call you back later." Then he turned to my husband and declared, "Edda must immediately resume her duties so as to set a good example." That is what I intended to do, but I had to wait for a new nurse's uniform.

Galeazzo did not understand how my father could be so phlegmatic about my having been in danger. He himself was in the habit of embracing his father or any other relative each time they met. And the same was true when he ran into one of his friends, even if their separation had been a short one. He wasn't affected or excessively sentimental but rather expansive and in need of feeling human warmth all around him. He also had a deep reverence for sincere friendship.

When he became a Cabinet Minister, he did everything possible to convince his childhood companions and his intimate friends, who had known him when he had not yet reached such a high position, that he had not changed and that they could always behave with him as before. And even when he went on an official trip to Livorno, where he had grown up, he always made certain that he would have time to call on his old school friends.

I do not believe that any of them who ever needed him did

not have the right to his immediate solicitude. He would go so far as to volunteer his services to avoid their suffering any embarrassment at being forced to take the first step.

Some well-intentioned minds have written that Galeazzo behaved in this fashion only in order to make his power felt and that mere vanity compelled him to render such service. Not only did I never see or feel the least condescension in his attitude, but he never boasted about having been of use to others. And in saying this, I am being truly objective.

For example, one day I told him that my former Jewish boyfriend and his father had been sent by the Italian authorities to a concentration camp, and I asked him to intervene. He did so immediately, not only to please me but also because he felt that they had done nothing against Italy and should be freed. He neither turned this act into an affair of state nor ever spoke of it again.

But this affability, which he readily displayed if his companion was pleasing, well groomed, and apparently intelligent, was not extended to all and sundry. Like all men, he had his "favorites," as well as those who did not please him for one reason or another, this sometimes owing to only a visceral dislike. I remember certain of our relatives whom we would meet on the golf course or at the home of mutual friends but whom we never received at our home because Galeazzo refused to do so.

He had great respect for people's feelings, and this may have struck some persons as mawkish or oversentimental. But to those who had known Galeazzo as a boy, such behavior was not at all surprising and their judgment, along with that of his parents, was much different. They knew that his comportment was based on the principles instilled in him by Costanzo and Carolina Ciano, which he had already put into practice at school.

Galeazzo's overscrupulous conscience, which made it so difficult for him to hurt anyone, caused him to be quite timorous about punishing or dismissing a servant. Therefore, I was the one who was forced to be "mean." He would explain to me what had occurred, sometimes in writing if I were away; then he would tell me what decision he had arrived at, and it would be up to me to apply that decision.

It has often been said that courageous men who confront danger and death without flinching are terrified of small bruises or minor illnesses. My husband was just like that. The moment he felt the slightest pain he believed that he was certainly going to die, and the slightest headache was instantly transformed by his imagination into a brain tumor. Once he even tried to convince me that a contagious illness could be caught on the telephone. I found this hilarious, especially since I had always felt that a little dust around the house was healthy because it inured one to microbes. When he fell ill, what a spectacle! And everyone knew of it, of that I can assure you.

I don't know which of the two, my father or my husband, was more of a mollycoddle. My father could not stand remaining in the room with someone who was coughing. He would immediately see the microbes spreading throughout the house, and when he was sick we were forbidden to cross the threshold of his bedroom. He who had suffered the worst tortures when he had been riddled with shrapnel during the First World War, who had crashed in his plane, who had one day been thrown from his car, and who had fought so many duels, became stiff with terror when he had to have an injection—in fact, one time he stiffened so much that the needle broke. It was equally difficult to give him medicine, and I remember an incident that remained famous in the family annals.

We were still living in Milan at the time, and my father had some medical treatment or other to follow. My grandmother, mother, and I had to put on a real performance! My mother filled the spoon, held it out to my father; then we three opened our mouths and said, "Ahhh!" while Papa swallowed the potion. I don't know what got into me that day, but seeing my father with his mouth gaping open in disgust after having taken the medicine, gave me the impulse to slap his face ever so lightly. We were both equally astounded by my gesture.

My father looked at me severely, pointed to one of the corners of the room, and said in a curt voice, "Stand in that corner for one hour!" Then he took his alarm clock, set it for an hour hence, and placed it on the table before him. We were both being punished, although he spent the time comfortably ensconced at table, eating a plate of lovely fried potatoes at which I stared longingly. That was, I believe, the only time that someone in the family had ever dared to raise a hand against my father.

I never would have dared to do such a thing to Galeazzo. First of all, I understood that I owed my husband too much respect to indulge in such a gesture; secondly, he would certainly not have exhibited the same gentleness as my father but would have immediately slapped me back—and hard!

It has been said that my husband was flighty and superficial. How can appearances be so misleading? It is true that his joviality might have passed for frivolity. But in fact I have never met a man so organized, so methodical, so punctilious in all domains.

With regard to our homes, for example, it was he who not only personally supervised the arrangements for our apartment in Rome and our prefabricated villa in Capri, but even watched carefully over the construction of the latter. He modified the architects' plans; he had fireplaces put in most of the rooms to make them cozy; he decided to have marble floors in our Rome apartment; he dispensed with the verandas because he found them to be a useless waste of space; and he saw to it that all the rooms were spacious and luxurious, equipped with comfortable, functional furniture. It was because of his impeccable taste that our homes were a pleasure to live in.

The layout of a house interested him to such an extent that sometimes, when we visited a place, he would mechanically measure in his mind the dimensions of a room as he entered it. And it was not unusual to see him walk up and down to survey the rooms so as to verify if his calculations were correct or not. With great precision, he could foresee exactly where the furniture should go, and I must admit that he was rarely wrong.

I do not know if such qualities are transmitted from generation to generation, but our children do seem to have inherited this talent of his, although they were very young when they lost their father. Fabrizio, Dindina (our nickname for Raimonda), and Marzio have always had furniture conceived specially for the place in which they wished to install it, and it is useless to look for a bookcase, a cabinet, or a table that is larger or smaller than the space it is to occupy in their rooms.

This care for detail was not limited to the setting up of our home but also extended to how the house actually worked, to its general administration. My father was quite the contrary and only paid attention to two things, which were, moreover, primordial in his eyes: he did not want to have anyone living above us because he had a horror of noise—which is why, before moving into the Villa Torlonia, we had always lived in an apartment situated on the top floor of the building—and he insisted on having the most possible free space and the least possible amount of furniture, so as to be able to stride around a room with ease. As soon as he would see a pouf, for example, he would kick it heartily and then it would disappear.

Galeazzo did not interest himself in our daily expenses: it was I who was in charge of that department and who established the budget for our cook. But he never once forgot to place the necessary money at my disposal, and I never had to ask for it. He demanded that the refrigerator always be full and the house ready to receive guests at any moment. The rugs had to remain unrolled and the furniture uncovered, even if we were away. Our wine cellar was always well furnished, for, though he was not a real connoisseur of wines and spirits, he wanted his table to be perfect from all points of view. And I must say that he was right, because experience has taught me that nothing leads to entertaining conversation and a delightful party better than a well-laden table, an agreeable ambiance, and pretty women dressed in lovely clothes.

During our stay in China, where Galeazzo was Consul General, then Chargé d'Affaires from 1930 to 1933, he used that procedure to reverse completely a bad situation that had arisen with an English journalist from Shanghai, a certain Woodhead, who had until then been extremely disagreeable with the Italians as well as others.

"We are going to invite Woodhead to the house and take very good care of him," said my husband. "You will see then how his attitude will change."

Woodhead came to dine at our Shanghai residence. The quality of the food and wine, my husband's amiability and my youthful high spirits, normal in a young woman of twenty, worked marvels. From that day on, Italy had no more ardent defender than Mr. Woodhead.

In his search for perfection, Galeazzo, in Shanghai as in Rome, chose the best cooks to be found. The only problem was that, being aware of their value, they did not deprive themselves of skimming good round sums from the budget to line their own pockets. And when things became too flagrant we were forced to call a halt to such practices.

One day, in Peking, Galeazzo discovered that we had used up seventy-five eggs in one week. He asked Jean, the cook, for an explanation. The latter replied with a grin that the *kam-shaw* (tip) that the personnel automatically took from the budget had risen considerably because they had seen a postcard from Livorno we had received and that represented the Palace Hotel located on a square bearing the name Costanzo Ciano. They had thus concluded that the large and handsome edifice belonged to us and that we had more revenue than most diplomats. Thus, the new "assessment."

Our Italian cook in Rome, who was more easily offended, had replied to a little note that I had given him, pointing out the increase in household expenses, with a letter full of all sorts of explanations and written on official notepaper.

My husband gave proof of the same meticulous temperament on the professional level as well. Even after his departure from the Ministry of Foreign Affairs, there remained a certain "Ciano" spirit, a certain turn of mind and way of administering the agency.

While he was Minister, Galeazzo never charged any of his personal expenditures to the Ministry, even if they might have entered quite legally into the expense-account ledger of the budget. We could, for example, have lived at the Villa Madama, the official residence, but instead we remained in our own home. We could have charged up our dinners and receptions at home to the Ministerial budget because of the people of consequence—foreign ambassadors and others—who attended them, but we did not do so. Galeazzo refused to use the expense account for anything other than the strictly official parties we gave at the Villa Madama itself.

And if a further proof of his scrupulous tendencies is needed, I could recall my husband's last hours in his prison cell at Scalzi before his execution. He consecrated those hours to writing letters and, above all, to drawing up his will, using all his clear-sightedness to ensure that neither I nor our children should be in want or difficulty after his death.

It has been asserted that Galeazzo Ciano was not a cultivated man, that the only polish he displayed had been acquired by him solely to please his father-in-law and his wife, that his intelligence was merely average. This statement is but one of the many inventions concerning Galeazzo that have been bruited about by our enemies, privately during the war and publicly when the war ended with the defeat of the Axis. When an important personage falls from a great height, then everyone rushes to attack him, to crush him underfoot.

Some historians have gone so far as to declare that our library existed only for show, that Galeazzo read barely at all and that I myself spent my reading time devouring American scandal sheets.

We were in sum, according to them, the perfect couple—he imbecilic and I trivial.

The truth was exactly the opposite. My husband was not only endowed with a lively intelligence that enabled him to understand situations with extreme rapidity and rare perspicacity, but he enjoyed an unparalleled sense of humor. I must admit that his humor was sometimes savage and must have often done him a disservice when certain of his important interlocutors learned that they had been its victim. . . .

As to his intellect, he had been a brilliant student and, even before meeting me, he had occupied several diplomatic posts. When we met he already spoke French, English, Spanish, and Portuguese as well as his native Italian. He began to learn Chinese during our stay in Shanghai, but more years were needed to make the results effective.

As to books, not only did we own them for other reasons than a pretty facade, but Galeazzo loved to read. His favorite authors were foreign, mostly French, but he also knew a great deal about Italian literature, history, and art; theater and music were a source of relaxation for him when he had the time to enjoy them.

I did like to read American magazines, but they were not at all my sole reading matter. I liked, and still like, detective stories, the great classics, the drama, and my bedside book was not the Bible or the Gospel but Voltaire or Wodehouse. Still today, I rarely go out without taking a book along with me. However, I do not have to show off my learning.

My husband's eclecticism encompassed various domains. He had taste in decoration, books, paintings, and jewels. He admired beautiful women and pretty clothes. He was a gourmet and extremely elegant. He was highly admired in the best Roman society and he was invited because he was Galeazzo Ciano rather than because he was the husband of Mussolini's daughter.

The only thing he lacked in my eyes was a propensity for sports. I think that my husband was the only member of the Mussolini and Ciano families who was not bitten by that bug. My father rode horseback, skied, fenced, swam, rode a motorcycle, et cetera. My brother Bruno introduced basketball to Italy. My other brother, Vittorio, played football, even with my father, to the chagrin of my mother and the misfortune of the windows of the Villa Torlonia; and for a certain period he was president of the European Boxing Federation. I myself adored acrobatics as well as swimming and horseback riding. Galeazzo considered sports as a health remedy, nothing more.

He did not like to drive, appreciated horseback riding only vaguely, and when he happened to take a few days of vacation at the seaside he was satisfied to swim only a few strokes and then lie on the beach in the sun. He did take out our sailboat—our sole yacht—but he was rather lazy as a skipper. I think I saw him swim like a fish only once: that was in Livorno in 1943 on a summer day. The city had been badly bombarded by the Allies. The port was in danger and our daughter, Dindina, was on a float. Galeazzo rushed out to bring her back to safety.

On the other hand, he did like golf. It was the only sport he ever practiced with passion. Some people have said that he played golf because it was snobbish to do so, but that is not true. He thought it was the only physical exercise that did not have the usual dull, tiresome, tedious side he found in most other exercises intended to maintain the figure. Also, the Golf Club in Rome was extremely agreeable, and many diplomats and industrialists liked to meet there because it was possible to talk seriously without being restrained by the solemn aspect of a Ministerial office.

But golf did not prove to offer enough exercise to compensate for Galeazzo's healthy appetite and his penchant for spaghetti. Sometimes he would leave the bathroom with a pensive air. "Have you noticed my double chin and the signs of a belly, Edda?" he would say. "I must do something about that!"

The "something" would be done immediately. Galeazzo would buy one or another sort of apparatus, whose virtues for ridding one of pounds had been extolled to him, but it would end by serving only to take up space in a room and to stub one's toe against. Then my husband would resume his old habit of accepting with a smile our jokes about his double chin, his budding stoutness, or his Chaplinesque walk.

I am not maintaining that Galeazzo Ciano was a perfect man. Obviously, he had his faults. His most important defect, on the personal level, was that he never took over a week or ten days of vacation at a stretch during our thirteen years of life together. He was too absorbed by his work to stay away from it to be with his wife and children for any greater length of time.

And though my husband was a celebrated and adulated Cabinet Minister, though I myself was blessed with tokens of homage and esteem, like all women I desired my husband's presence. We women feel the need of that presence to maintain our precious equilibrium. And that my husband never understood.

VIII

It was in 1932, while we were living in China, that Galeazzo first felt the effects of the asthma that was to make him suffer until the end of his life. The asthma attacks affected his ears, necessitating several operations, and at times the pain he endured was so intolerable that he was forced to sit for a while with his mouth wide open, taking deep breaths in order to dissipate a temporary deafness.

This made him look rather amusing, and one day, upon seeing him open his mouth, I had the stupid idea of imitating him, which gave the impression that I was making fun of him. I had no sooner made a vague movement of my lips than I felt an object graze my head. My husband had just thrown an ashtray in my face, missing me only by inches—and, I might add, he did not regret his faulty aim.

This incident has only an anecdotal value, but in itself it is very significant: it shows that Galeazzo Ciano was as capable of being stung to anger by me as by anyone else. Moreover, I would not have had it otherwise. I was much more submissive to my husband than my mother was to hers.

After our marriage I slept for several months covered with blankets, in a room whose windows were hermetically closed, because my husband was in the habit of sleeping like that. It was only on board the ship taking us to China that I rebelled for the first time. It was difficult to endure being covered with blankets in the month of September while sleeping in a ship's cabin whose portholes were closed and ventilators turned off.

Therefore, after two days at sea, I gave Galeazzo an ultimatum: "If you do not open the ventilators, I will change cabins!"

"But I cannot sleep any other way," he replied. So, I changed cabins.

Some people might think Galeazzo a cad for having behaved in that fashion. But I was not offended. He wished to be at ease, so did I, and we had found the solution. And after all, what difference did it make, since we were able to be together as much as we liked.

My husband was the head of the household from the very start of our marriage, and I never tried to oppose his authority. Such behavior would have been impossible, in any case, for he was always quick to anger and of an extremely jealous nature, so that it was the better part of valor not to provoke him.

I had occasion to perceive this one day in May or June of 1934. We were in the habit of going to Castel Fusano, a section of the beach at Ostia, near Rome. Galeazzo would work in the capital every morning and join me at the beach for lunch. I had decided to inaugurate a new bathing suit that I had brought back from England. The suit was a two-piece affair, and between the top and the bottom a glimpse of flesh could be caught. At that time such an outfit was as shocking as a topless suit would be today.

Foreseeing the savage reaction of my husband if he were to find me wearing this immodest bathing suit, I convinced the wife of Alighiero Giovanelli, a close friend of my husband's, to buy one also, so that Galeazzo could see that I was not the only one to dare appear in it.

Usually Galeazzo and Alighiero would arrive at the beach at about 1:30 P.M. But that day they were early, and we had not had enough time to change and welcome them in more "chaste" outfits, which was what we had been doing for the previous week. As soon as we had greeted each other my husband said to me coldly, "Come to our bathhouse for a moment. I have something to say to you."

As soon as we were alone, he shouted, "How can you exhibit yourself like that in public?" And then he slapped me hard— twice, as a matter of fact.

I could only reply, "But I'm not the only one. Lola is wearing one too."

"I don't give a damn! I forbid you to dress like that! Take that suit off immediately and change into a more decent one!"

When I came out of the bathhouse, my friend Lola was not on the beach. And when she did appear, she also was wearing a different suit.

I must add that the other women on the beach had seen our suits before our husbands' arrival, and several days later, as if by magic, they blossomed forth all over the beach.

Incidents such as the above did not occur frequently, because Galeazzo and I had fortunately begun to know and understand each other rather well. Our viewpoints were so similar that when he carried on a flirtation he generally had the good taste to choose his partner from among my most attractive and likable friends.

It is true that it took me some time to be serene about those flirtations. I even thought of leaving him, but I decided against it after examining my innermost feelings and after a conversation with my father at his office in the Palazzo Venezia.

"Papa," I said, "I want to leave Galeazzo."

My father looked at me searchingly. "Why? Doesn't he give you enough to eat? Does he leave you without enough money or let you lack for something?"

"Oh, no, it's not that."

"Then, is he unfaithful?"

"Perhaps."

"Are you in love with someone else?"

"Not at all!"

"Then go home, and let's hear no more of this nonsense!"

The discussion ended there. My father obviously felt that it was up to me to settle my affairs on my own. My parents behaved in this reserved way with all their children and never interfered in their personal lives.

When Vittorio decided to marry, my father made no objection. He and my mother presided over the festivities in a hotel (rather than at home, as my mother had not forgotten how much work my wedding had entailed) and that was all. I believe that my father never even visited their home.

When it was Bruno's turn to marry, he had only one worry: Gina, his fiancée, was very dark, and our mother abhorred brunettes. Bruno asked me for advice, and I replied that he should tell Gina to dye her hair blond and Mother wouldn't notice anything. Papa straightened out the matter of the color of Gina's hair with Mama, but he interfered no more in their personal affairs. As far as I know, he went to their house only once. And he came to our home only two or three times during our married life—on the occasion of the birth of my children.

This does not mean that my father was not interested in us but simply that he wished to leave us in peace, just as he wished for himself.

Galeazzo was an excellent father, who adored his children, even though he was very severe with them about high principles and good manners. Early in our marriage I had wanted many children, but I changed my mind quickly after the birth of the first and declared that we would have only one. However, despite this affirmation, we then had Dindina, whom I also called "the mistake," poor little thing, and Marzio, whom we called Mowgli or "the child of reason." And thank goodness we had no more after that!

Like all fathers, Galeazzo preferred his daughter. If he had lived longer, I think that he would have behaved with her as my father had with me.

Ciccino (our nickname for Fabrizio, the older boy) was treated with more severity than his sister. Mowgli was too young to be disciplined as yet. Galeazzo applied to Ciccino the methods of his own father. The naval officer resurfaced, and it was not a rare occurrence to see Ciccino stand at attention before his father when he had behaved foolishly or done something wrong and stoically await the slaps that he deserved. Then he would return to his room and remain there until the punishment had ended.

I was sorry for him, but I couldn't and wouldn't, in any case, interfere. Someone in the house had to be the disciplinarian. And I represented the humorous element in the family; I was the one to play with them, to tell them stories and jokes, to dance with them. In sum, I was merely their elder sister—"the fourth of my children," my husband would say.

Galeazzo represented the stable element, the head of the family, who seemed to lack whimsy and was severe because that was required by his role. This does not imply that he was not extremely attentive and considerate with the children. When school opened each year he arranged to be free and in Rome, no matter what his obligations might be, and, looking very dignified indeed, he carried his children's schoolbags and accompanied them to school. This ceremony never varied or was interrupted until his untimely death.

Sometimes Dindina remembers certain anecdotes, and nothing is more poignant to me than to hear her recount them. The other day she recalled to me that, during an official ceremony, she and her brother Ciccino each led a gymnastic team that had been chosen to execute certain rhythmic movements as their part of the performance given at that celebration.

They were extremely proud because their father, at that time the Minister of Foreign Affairs, was presiding over the celebration. Though Ciccino could make his young comrades execute practically perfect movements without the least difficulty, unfortunately Dindina only achieved a handsome mess with her group for, having never known how to distinguish her right side from her left, she did exactly the opposite of what she ordered her comrades to do. That is to say, when she ordered them to turn right, she turned left. And when she wished to repair her error and turned in the direction taken by her teammates, she found herself face to face with those who were trying to follow her. This brought about a disorder that panicked her completely.

She told me that Galeazzo, standing in the official box, had been amused by her difficulties in the beginning. Then, realizing that she was very upset, he began to suffer for her and, despite the solemnity of the occasion, he tried to help her. Each time that Dindina gave an order, with a discreet signal of his hand, her father would indicate the direction in which she should turn and thus, by following Galeazzo's gestures, my daughter ended her performance more brilliantly than she had begun it.

His obvious affection for Dindina did not prevent Galeazzo from administering her a vigorous pair of slaps in the face several days after that celebration because, affectionate sister that she was, she dared come to the defense of her older brother, who was being punished once again. Her father completely lost his temper when she shouted at him, *"Tu sei un fesso"* ("You are a bloody imbecile"), an impropriety of language that my husband could not tolerate.

Galeazzo was uncompromising about any lack of decorum, and I heard him swear only once or twice during our fourteen years together—when he was truly beside himself with rage.

His father, Costanzo, like all good sailors, did not hesitate to use a swear word when it would strengthen a phrase or had a bearing on what he was trying to express. It was amusing to hear my mother-in-law, Carolina, pick up those phrases and use certain "old salt" expressions in chic drawing rooms, sowing consternation among all the affected, priggish ladies who were cautiously nibbling at their biscuits and taking care to crook their little finger when drinking their tea.

To this intransigence respecting impropriety of language, Galeazzo added another—our children were not to be involved in any way in our quarrels. I shared this point of view unreservedly, and it had much to do with their subsequent poise and stability.

They lived in an apartment beneath ours, with their nurse. Our own way of life never disturbed theirs, at least not until 1943–1944, when destiny took over and we became helpless.

IX

"WHEN I GO OUT, I LIKE TO RELAX, TO MEET ATTRACTIVE AND agreeable people, to see lovely women wearing beautiful clothes," Galeazzo remarked. Contrary to my father, who appreciated women only as a physical outlet, my husband enjoyed them for esthetic reasons also. I do not mean to imply that he was a saint and without reproach in this regard, but merely that he was not an obsessed male who constantly ran after them and could not see a woman without indulging in a breach of good manners. Nevertheless, Joseph Kennedy, after having met Galeazzo in 1933 or '34, declared:

"I have never met such a pompous and vain imbecile. He spent most of his time talking about women and spoke seriously to no one, for fear of losing sight of the two or three girls he was running after. I left him with the conviction that we would have obtained more from him by sending him a dozen pretty girls rather than a group of diplomats."

I sincerely believe that Mr. Kennedy's opinion was absolutely wrong, as false as all those rumors and newspaper articles that described me as a Messalina, a debauched woman who liked to visit Germany, for example, to sleep with the Führer's personal guards because they were tall, blond, and handsome.

There were also stories recounting that the social life of the upper classes under the Fascist regime was spent in debauchery, which sometimes led to scandal, at the beach and in the mountains.

Some unimportant incidents did, of course, occur in the diplomatic life of the capital, as they do everywhere. For instance, the wife of a British diplomat was caught in the act in a hotel in Rome with a young Italian. Her husband was discreetly recalled to London upon the intervention of my father when he was informed about it.

It is also true that sometimes at Cortina d'Ampezzo there were rows between people who were slightly excited by alcohol. One day in 1937 I had to intervene with the police of that locality to free some gentlemen who had passed the night in jail after a bout of fisticuffs. Everyone was amused at the time of this episode because it was a rare experience for such people to pass the night behind bars. But neither my father nor my husband thought it a laughing matter, and I had to endure a fine scolding from Galeazzo for having become involved in it.

But this does not signify that the *dolce vita* under Fascism was any more spicy than it is today or had been in previous times. Also, I don't see why people shouldn't have had a good time under Mussolini's rule. But my father was inclined to a certain austerity, and if it had been up to him there would have been no *dolce vita* either in wartime or in peacetime. I remember our having one of our most violent arguments on this subject.

It was during the war, and we were at Riccione. My father began to rail against the free-and-easy behavior of some people who dared to dance and have a gay time while the country was at war. I reacted very sharply, maintaining that it was quite normal for soldiers and nurses like me to need some relaxation in order to forget the horrors of war upon returning from the Front. I reminded him that many soldiers had been on dangerous missions, during which they had barely escaped death, and that, in any case, they were perhaps going to lose their lives when they returned to combat.

My father upheld the contrary thesis, declaring that combatants' nerves should remain taut and their will should not be weakened by dances and other sophisticated pleasures. I rejoined that dancing and enjoying oneself could hardly be classified as "sophisticated." Papa continued to disagree with me. I finally asserted that I found his reasoning specious, that I shared the life of the soldiers and knew what I was talking about. We both stormed and shouted, and when Papa left the room he slammed the door so hard that pieces of plaster fell from the wall.

Galeazzo and I spent not particularly novel evenings together, and, except for vacations, we were practically never alone for dinner. We ate out at other people's homes or at embassies several times a week, and on the other evenings we either gave a dinner party at our apartment on the Via Angelo Secchi when no protocol was involved, or else an official dinner at the Villa Madama.

Galeazzo would usually try to return home from the office so that we could have some relaxed moments with the children, but there were times when he found it necessary to change at his office and then I would pick him up at the Ministry.

It might appear that it must have been considered a fine thing to have Mussolini's daughter and her husband as guests. That was not so, really, and except for the parties organized by personal friends, the invitations were always addressed to Galeazzo Ciano and his wife rather than to Edda Mussolini and her husband. As a matter of fact, the people whom we did not know intimately took for granted that, given the close relationship I had with my father, I might keep him informed of what was said or done in the salons around Rome.

Our hosts were mistaken, for not only did I not care a fig for all the little intimate gossip that so enchanted my husband, but I behaved exactly like everyone else, drinking English whisky and smoking American contraband cigarettes. The only time I informed my father of what had occurred in a drawing room, the story concerned a party that I had not attended.

I had just returned from the Front, when I was told that a reception had been given in honor of an American diplomat who was leaving Rome following the break in diplomatic relations between Italy and the United States.

I was astounded and furious: astounded to discover that there were certain persons who had so much social vanity that they dared to give a reception when our country was at war and austerity should have been practiced by everyone; furious because I could not understand how they could have so stupidly compromised their guests, whose patriotism could not be doubted but who, having accepted this invitation, risked being dragged into political and police complications that did not really concern them. And the latter was unavoidable because the diplomat, now regarded as an enemy, was escorted at all times by plainclothesmen whose mission it was to protect him as well as to keep a close eye on his activities until his departure. It is obvious that they made lists of the guests for use by the Ministry of the Interior.

Although I had protested against the gloomy climate that my father had wished to impose on those soldiers who had risked their lives for their country, I was outraged by such unpatriotic and frivolous behavior by these people, despite the fact that the diplomat in question was personally a fine man. So I went to see my father and actually demanded sanctions.

To return to our social life, I would say that among the salons in Rome in which we were most often received, the two most popular were those of Princess Isabella Colonna and of Countess Pecci-Blunt.

Princess Colonna's salon was famous above all because of her extraordinary personality. Her maiden name was Sursok, and she

89

came from the Middle East, which seemed most exotic at the time. Her husband was Marc-Antonio Colonna, who bore a historic name as his family had furnished Italy with popes, cardinals, and generals from the thirteenth to the seventeenth centuries. Both enjoyed large fortunes and thus were able to give divinely luxurious parties, attended by all the Italian and even European celebrities. Though she had taken on Italian nationality upon her marriage, Isabella Colonna never lost her Middle Eastern sense of intrigue, her art of knowing about everything, and she had no equal for revealing a secret or making up a story of her own with those dangerous words: "So and so told me that . . ."

Galeazzo noted in his notebooks on December 25, 1941, after the Pope's speech, which had not pleased Papa at all: "Isabella Colonna informed me last night that she had spoken recently with Cardinal Maglione [Secretary of State at the Holy See] who told her that at the Vatican they preferred the Russians to the Nazis . . ."

Across the kaleidoscope that was her salon, if one listened carefully, it was possible to know what was "in" and what was "out," who was in favor and who was in disgrace. And as she did not take the trouble to mince words, Isabella's conversational gossip was extremely amusing, especially since her critical faculties were highly polished. For these reasons, her invitations were particularly sought after.

It was said that the true Ministry of Foreign Affairs, during Ciano's time, was not the Palazzo Chigi but the Palazzo Colonna, the latter situated, moreover, only several hundred meters away. Isabella and my husband were extremely close, and there is no doubt that he confided in her. But I believe that Isabella's affection for Galeazzo prevented her from ever harming him by spreading hasty gossip gleaned from what he told her. True he was Foreign Minister of one of the most powerful nations in Europe, but his comments were, of necessity, not always political either. Their complicity was total. Not only did she regale him with the gossip of which he was so fond, but she also arranged encounters or dinners with women who happened to catch his fancy.

I reacted against this only once, when Isabella gave a dinner for an actress who was rather famous at the time and who was admired by Galeazzo. I did not attend that dinner, for I was not always clinging to my husband's shirttails and enjoyed my own personal affairs. But I was shocked that Isabella Colonna and her guests had consorted with an actress. At that time theater and film people had not yet been taken up in our milieu, unlike what happens today, and I felt that Isabella had gone too far, even though she had done so only to please Galeazzo. When I told him what I thought he was merely amused, and the scene ended in gales of laughter on both sides.

The second most popular salon was the sole literary and artistic salon in Italy. It was, as I have said, that of Countess Pecci-Blunt, whom we called "Mimi." Her destiny was as strange and happy as that of Isabella. Her great-uncle was Gioacchino Pecci, Pope Leo XIII, who gave his imprint to the history of Christianity by an encyclical, *Rerum novarum,* that favored penetration of the world of the workers by the Church and excited world interest concerning modern society.

Despite this celebrated ancestry, Mimi did not seem happy. Although cultivated, intelligent, and from a very good family, she did not have a great deal of money and was obliged to work to earn her living, which was extremely rare at that time in a milieu like hers. She had reached thirty-two or -three without having found a kindred spirit, when she met Cecil Blumenthal, a wealthy American of Jewish origin.

When they decided to marry, an obstacle appeared in their way: Although American and rich, Mr. Blumenthal was a Jew, and that was awkward since his wife-to-be was the great-niece of a Pope. By means of a sleight-of-hand that can happen in situations of this kind, Cecil Blumenthal was soon transformed into Cecil Blunt, which betrayed his origins much less. Then Cecil Blunt was ennobled by a papal decision—the Pope was, I believe, Benedict XV. Profiting from this occasion, Cecil had his name changed once again by adding that of Pecci, and as Count Pecci-Blunt he was thus able to become a proper husband for Mimi Pecci, the great-niece of a Pope, without provoking the least sarcastic remark.

Far from behaving like a nouveau riche who ostentatiously shows off her fortune, Mimi Pecci-Blunt chose to become a Mycenas and promote the arts. She built a small theater that continued to function even after the war—Mimi died only last year—and she opened her doors to intellectuals. We met writers, journalists, and musicians at her home, and the concerts were very advanced for the time as they concentrated for the most part on the new twelve-tone music.

Mimi's receptions and dinners had only one drawback—the food was terrible. Galeazzo, referring to the hostess's papal ancestor, nicknamed her table the "table of the Borgias." And in order to avoid tasting the dishes, he proclaimed that he could eat only canned food, slipped several cans to the butler when he came to dine, and was happy to have their contents served to him separately. Not daring to follow his example, I merely took the advice of the butler, who would whisper in my ear when he served me, "Do not take this course, Excellency. Wait for the other one, which is better."

Mimi never became offended by Galeazzo's behavior at dinners because, just as with Isabella, he was her pet and she excused everything he did. I truly wasn't at all vexed by the special attentions Galeazzo enjoyed from these ladies and others. I placed myself well above such childishness. He could amuse himself as he wished, and I didn't mind. When I wished I took part, and when I didn't feel like it I didn't accompany him.

Galeazzo had the tact and delicacy never to demand that I accompany him when he knew that I did not want to do so. And he never obliged me to receive certain persons whom I did not want to meet. I must also say that none of Galeazzo's mistresses ever placed me in an embarrassing position. I cannot say whether this was because my husband, who knew how to distinguish between an affair and a marriage, would not have tolerated it or because I was Mussolini's daughter and my temperamental character was well known. But one thing is certain: except for those periods when I was pregnant and therefore victimized by complexes, my pride never suffered—except once.

The only thing that I had to reproach Galeazzo with was his unfortunate tendency to talk too much and too openly. He didn't reveal state secrets—he had too great a sense of responsibility for that. But, during an evening, he was likely to make a comment about a situation or an event that had just occurred or that he foresaw would come to pass. Or he would lash out against a general or marshal or minister who had not adequately performed his job, or against our German allies, his favorite targets, among whom was Joachim von Ribbentrop, the Reich's Minister of Foreign Affairs.

Those observations would probably have been of no importance if they had been uttered by an underling and would perhaps not have been prejudicial to the person who made them. But Galeazzo was the Foreign Minister and the son-in-law of Il Duce, as well as his "heir" (according to some rumors), which gave his comments added importance and aroused much interest.

Conscious of the risks such pleasantries or confidences in a salon could involve, and perhaps also because of my natural reserve, I often warned Galeazzo to be careful of giving away secrets or making statements he might not wish repeated. My husband declared that he was prudent, and this was true in general. However, I am convinced that he was often careless when he confided in people, especially when he spoke with pretty women, and that some of his remarks were repeated either to the Germans or to the Fascist extremists.

My father never mentioned this subject to me, but he must have known all about it. He apparently gave Galeazzo's remarks no more importance than he would have accorded to any salon conversation. Perhaps, also, it suited him to have this irreverent critic beside him, a critic whose fidelity he knew he could rely on and who could serve as a "safety valve." This is merely a hypothesis, but it might well explain my father's silence about the matter. Unless, that is, he simply did not dare to face me with his objections.

X

I DO NOT BELIEVE THAT MY HUSBAND WAS EITHER A NONENTITY
or a Machiavelli, and still less a traitor. It is true, however, that,
if he had been free to do so, he would have carried out a completely different policy from my father's. You must remember that
Galeazzo Ciano was only Foreign Minister. This means, as is the
case in all governments, that he had to obey his head of state,
in this instance Mussolini, and follow his directives.

From a certain period on, there was a definite conflict of personalities between my husband and my father, a conflict that
became a terrible dilemma for Galeazzo and lay at the bottom
of his tragic drama. Once he no longer shared my father's opinions
about foreign policy Galeazzo should logically have resigned.
But in the beginning events made it seem that my father might
be right, so that Galeazzo feared he had been mistaken, and then,

when events proved Galeazzo to be right, Italy was far too involved as an ally of Germany and could no longer draw back. Furthermore, any inopportune gesture on Galeazzo's part, such as resignation, would have irremediably harmed the administration of the country, for the political conflict would have been exacerbated by the addition of a family controversy. And, finally, it is difficult to drop the reins of power when one has held them as Minister of Foreign Affairs since the age of thirty-three.

My mother always maintained that if my father-in-law, Costanzo Ciano, had not died in 1939, the events that occurred in 1943 and afterward would not have taken place. She meant that Mussolini would not have been repudiated on July 24, 1943, and then arrested on July 25. This does not imply that Italy would not have been defeated by the formidable power of the Allies, but the country would at least have avoided being disunited and thus almost torn to pieces.

I cannot swear that Costanzo could have avoided the events that occurred, but I am certain that he would not have allowed the domestic situation to deteriorate as it did. Also, he would surely have reacted differently after the vote of the Inner Council.

When the Socialist deputy, Giacomo Matteotti, was assassinated by the Fascist extremists on June 10, 1924, my father had been Premier for under two years. Caught between the right-wing faction of his party and his personal desire to maintain a liberal parliamentary regime, he felt helpless and at a loss. Public opinion and the majority of the parliamentarians saw in him the instigator of the crime. Several Ministers thought of resigning, and he himself wondered if he could continue to lead the country.

It was Costanzo Ciano who helped him to surmount this grave crisis. A hero of the First World War, and thus famous before the advent of Fascism, he took things in hand and not only vouched for my father's good faith but helped him to recover his serenity and lucidity. From that time on, a climate of confidence was established between him and my father, who stated in writing that Costanzo Ciano was to be his official successor if he, Mussolini, should disappear.

He became the only person in the regime who could face up to my father and stand his ground when that was necessary. His particularly strong personality was a fine complement to his absolute fidelity and made it possible for him to see clearly, within the framework of the Fascist regime, what was best for Italy. In short, Costanzo Ciano was my father's confidential agent on the domestic-policy front just as my paternal uncle Arnaldo Mussolini was in the realm of private affairs. Unfortunately, Arnaldo died in 1931 and Costanzo in 1939.

After 1939 there remained no outstanding men who could stand up to my father. His personality overwhelmed all he came into contact with, whether they were his collaborators, Fascists who did not see him very often, or foreign personalities. Gandhi, who so admirably understood the human mind and soul, and Churchill, a brilliant psychological maneuverer of statesmen, were both subjugated by Mussolini.

He was quite susceptible to anyone who was clever about influencing him, but there were few who really knew how to accomplish this. Very often it was the last person he had spoken to whom he would deem to be right about an issue. Many times people who had clear ideas about certain questions, and were convinced that their arguments were irrefutable, would enter his immense and imposing office, affirming that this time they would bring him around to their way of thinking, only to leave without having succeeded in making him share their point of view and even convinced that he was right! They were aware, certainly, that my father had maneuvered them, but that knowledge would come sometime later, long after they had left his presence.

Galeazzo Ciano was like these latter people. More than once he had crossed the threshold of Il Duce's office, determined to dot the *i*'s when he did not share the latter's views, especially in matters of foreign policy. But most of the time he left him in a

97

state of disarray, his views completely altered by Mussolini's arguments. And this despite the fact that my husband was one of those rare people, if not the only one, to meet my father several times a day and to have occasionally succeeded in making him share his opinion about important affairs of state.

I have often read in newspaper articles and books dealing with my father or my husband that Galeazzo Ciano had been appointed Foreign Minister only because he was Mussolini's son-in-law. That is not only false, but it shows how little they knew my father. The Mussolinis have always refused to indulge in nepotism.

My mother, for example, has a sister who is still living. They have not seen each other for forty years, and even today it is tacitly understood that we do not speak of my maternal aunt. This is because of the fact that my aunt once asked my mother for a special favor when my father was in power, and my mother refused. My aunt has never forgiven that refusal and my mother has never forgotten what still seems to her an indecent request.

Another example: One day in 1942, when I was a nurse on the Russian Front near Stalingrad, we had a visit from an Italian unit on leave from the front lines. I discovered with stupefaction that the cook was my cousin.

"What are you doing here as a cook?" I asked him.

"I have no idea," he replied. "I asked your mother to use her influence for me and this is the result! I do the cooking on the Russian Front!"

My own brothers can be cited as an example of this antinepotism of the Mussolini family.

When he was called by the King to head the government in 1922 my father named his brother Arnaldo to succeed him at the helm of his own newspaper, *Popolo d'Italia*. Arnaldo died of a heart attack in December of 1931, following the death of his son Sandro sixteen months before. My brother Vittorio, who had a certain talent and also quite a bit of experience as a journalist, would have been capable of heading the paper after a training period and with the assistance of several older persons, and he would have faithfully reflected my father's ideas. But Papa chose my cousin Vito Mussolini, son of uncle Arnaldo, to be the new director. He remained at that post until 1944 when my father ordered the paper sold because of the increasing pressures inflicted by the Germans and the Fascist extremists, and also because he felt that what had been his standard-bearer for thirty years had no more reason for existence.

Why did Mussolini choose his nephew over his own son? First, because my brother was still very young, and secondly, perhaps he felt it natural to give *Popolo* to Arnaldo's son since Arnaldo had been its director.

So you can see that Galeazzo had to prove himself before occupying a responsible post in the government, even though his mission to China had been crowned with success.

Thus, on our return from China in 1933, my husband found himself awaiting an assignment, that is to say without a definite position. For anyone but Galeazzo Ciano, to be a career diplomat, to have Il Duce as father-in-law, and to live in Rome with nothing to do all day would be a blessing. But Galeazzo was only thirty, he had just spent three years abroad, and he knew that he was capable of doing great things. He burned with impatience and grumbled constantly. "I'm fed up! If only I could work at something and use my mind. This is hell!"

I finally went to see my father, making the sole intervention of our life together—except for the time when I intervened unsuccessfully to save Galeazzo's life at the end.

"Listen," I said, "do what you wish. Send him where you wish But for goodness' sake, give him some work to do. He's had enough of loafing, and he's absolutely right."

Only two months had passed since our return from China, and my father could very well have replied that Galeazzo should be patient. But I was pregnant for the second time, not feeling well at all, and was considering the idea of moving back home. I wonder if the idea of having his domestic habits upset, and of other difficulties that this might entail, did not convince him to do something about my husband.

My father agreed that Galeazzo might do very well in an important post, but he still maintained that he must first prove his worth, son-in-law or no. So, after having been sent on a mission to London, Galeazzo was appointed Director of Press and Propaganda for the Premier's office. This position placed him in constant contact with the intricate machinery of the various wheels of government, and at the same time my father was given a chance to gauge his capabilities. Knowing that my husband had been a journalist and had enjoyed that profession several years earlier, Papa gave him the opportunity to steep himself once again in that ambiance and renew his useful ties with the newspaper world.

It was only after he had measured Galeazzo's capacity that Mussolini appointed him Secretary of State for Press and Propaganda when that department of the Ministry of Culture was transformed into a Secretariat. And when Galeazzo became Minister of Foreign Affairs for Italy on June 9, 1936, it was due to the fact that Il Duce deemed him capable of assuming such functions— and I counted for nothing in his decision.

Actually, having seen my husband's work in China, I knew that he was equal to any task. Unfortunately, China is far from Rome so that the historians have never been able to judge him properly for his work there, and at that time even my father was unaware of his true excellence.

The functions of the Consul General in Shanghai could have been a sinecure in the beginning. Relations with Chiang Kai-shek's China were good, but they did not have the same degree of importance in 1930 as our relations with France, England, Germany, and America, nations with interesting economic outlets. However, there was a market in China, and Italy owed it to itself to play a role in the face of France and England, who had divided between themselves the monopoly of commerce and political influence in that region of Asia.

The Chinese mentality and the division of power in the country were such that only personal relations with the different provincial governors, veritable satraps who had only remote administrative relations with Chiang Kai-shek, could allow Italy to hold its own with the great powers.

My husband did not move mountains, but he did a great deal to consolidate our relations with the Chinese authorities and to give a good image of Italy to the representatives of other countries as well as to the foreign press. Watching him at work, I understood how great were his talents for diplomacy and his faculty for grasping problems and people's psychology.

He was, of course, aided by the fact that this was his second stay in China, as he had already resided there as Secretary of the Legation; but Italy had changed since then. My father had by now surmounted his earlier difficulties and the policy of the Italian government had become resolutely dynamic.

My husband and I began by giving an impression of dynamism to our residence, our daily life, and our relations with everyone. Our Shanghai residence was completely renovated and our door was constantly open to guests. We behaved quite differently from the representatives of other countries, who were mostly older and often near the end of their diplomatic career, and thus less enthusiastic and more careful to economize in their budget.

This mode of behavior was extremely successful with the Chinese, who, contrary to the Japanese, who were rather formal and reserved, were soon intimate and agreeable friends. I was sometimes surprised by them, like the morning when I saw the Chinese Foreign Minister shaving in my husband's bathroom. Passing through Shanghai, he had come by to say hello to Galeazzo and had profited from his visit by washing up. I learned also not to be surprised if a well-known person telephoned to announce that he would not be coming to dinner with his wife but with his concubine. This was not a sign of unwarranted familiarity or bad taste but simply a manifestation of friendship.

In the spring of 1932 I succeeded in carrying off a brilliant commercial operation in the face of all the foreign diplomats—who were quite annoyed with me for some time. It occurred after a dinner that Chang Hsueh-liang, the strong man of the regime who was nicknamed "The Young Marshal," offered in Peking in honor of a commission of the League of Nations at the close of the Sino-Japanese conflict in Shanghai. Chang was governor of three of the most important Chinese provinces—Manchuria, Jehol, and Peking—and thus a most powerful person whose friendship was greatly in demand.

I was placed facing Chang at table. Toward the end of the meal he sent me a little note asking me to visit the Summer Palace with him on the following day. I accepted, and for several hours one of the most important men in China acted as my guide and kept Ministers and other important persons waiting while he walked with me. Naturally, that was very agreeable for my ego. The following month we saw each other in Peking and became close friends—Chang, his wife, his concubine, Galeazzo, and I.

One day, while we were discussing the Sino-Japanese conflict that had destroyed several provinces by that time and was menacing Manchuria, I demanded of Chang Hsueh-liang, "But you told me that you need planes. Why don't you buy them from Italy? We have excellent machines, which have beaten several records."

"Would your country sell them to me?"

"Why not?"

"Then it's an agreement. I shall order three."

Our conversation took place in English, which I spoke very well because of my lessons, my bridge parties, and the wives of British diplomats with whom I had been acquainted for the past year and a half in China. When I announced the news to Galeazzo he was skeptical, but we discovered that the three planes had actually been ordered from Italy. This almost caused a crisis with the French and the Americans, who had wanted to sell their own planes to Chang.

We accomplished another feat on the psychological and international level during the Sino-Japanese conflict. The fighting was taking place at the gates of Shanghai, and the foreign diplomats began to evacuate their families. But I decided that a diplomat's wife should remain with her husband to give an example, and I refused to budge. To be perfectly honest, I admit that I also wanted to see what was going to happen.

Galeazzo would have preferred to see me in a safe place, but he agreed to keep me with him. I had a great success in the press because all the papers spoke about the Count and Countess Ciano's act of courage. My photo appeared in the British newspaper of Shanghai along with the following caption: "The First Lady of Shanghai refuses to leave the city." That was the work of Woodhead.

Galeazzo reprimanded me more than once for visiting the sections of the city where fighting was going on. I was fascinated as I watched the operations of the "ronin," those admirably armed and disciplined Japanese fighters whose distinctive mark was a white headband worn over their forehead and wound round their head. The Chinese soldiers facing them were sad to see with their out-of-date arms, wearing shoes with holes—or even in bare feet—and uniforms that existed in name only; they fought without enthusiasm and some even carried an umbrella so as not to get wet if it rained.

Galeazzo enjoyed the first important satisfaction of his career at the end of that conflict. The youngest Chargé d'Affaires at the Shanghai Consulate, and the only one to remain, he was designated to direct the control commission of the League of Nations, mentioned above, which was charged with settling the conflict. He was chosen, though only twenty-nine, solely because he was capable. Not much publicity was given that mission. My father merely sent him a letter, saying in substance: "You did very good work. You have increased Italy's prestige abroad."

Living in China for three years was both fascinating and enriching. I discovered that China, which seemed to us Europeans slightly backward compared to our Latin civilization, was, in many areas, really in advance of our old continent by ten or fifteen years.

The neon signs that we came to know in Europe only after the Second World War were already lighting the Shanghai streets in 1930. There was air conditioning in the cinemas and I drank my first Coca-Cola in China.

Chinese customs, philosophy, civilization, although bewildering, were a constant source of joy to me. I discovered that it was possible to live in a more liberal fashion than in Europe while respecting other people's opinions even more, on the religious as well as on the social level. And to discover that mysterious country's art, history, and the hectic life of its streets was a marvelous adventure.

Finally, during the three years that we lived outside Italy, we were able to be truly ourselves. And far from the presence of our parents, comforting perhaps but a bit of a nuisance as well, my first child was born without all the confusion and hubbub that would certainly have taken place in Italy on the occasion of the confinement of Il Duce's daughter.

I must not forget to speak of Galeazzo's sense of humor and serenity when faced with certain situations, so as to complete the portrait of him that I discovered in China. One day, for example, I addressed him the following telegram from Pei Tai-ho: THE WORST HAS HAPPENED! STOP. HAVE LOST 4000 MEXICAN DOLLARS AT POKER. STOP. AM GOING TO KILL MYSELF. He replied with another telegram: HAVE SENT YOU 4000 DOLLARS. STOP. DON'T KILL YOURSELF. BAD IDEA. NOT WORTH IT. STOP.

In May, 1933, after two years and eight months in China, we returned to Italy. I must say that it needed an official wire from Papa to Galeazzo to convince us to leave. Papa had made several attempts to recall us, and we remained deaf to them until Galeazzo received what was an order from the head of government to one of his subordinate functionaries.

My husband had left Italy as Consul General; he returned after having brilliantly performed his duties as Chargé d'Affaires.

He was now an experienced diplomat who knew just how good he was. I had left Rome a young wife; I returned with a child in my arms and expecting another—which made me furious!

I was furious to have been forced to leave that spellbinding, magical country and to be pregnant again only two years after the birth of my first child. During our last days in Shanghai, I had been too busy to think of all that, but once aboard ship I realized that the fascinating life I had led for almost three years had now reached an end.

I had only to put away in a memory closet the names and faces of all the friends we had made during our stay, such as the British diplomats and their wives, whose bridge parties and teas accompanied by their unchanging biscuits were such fun. I became immediately nostalgic for the Russian restaurants in Shanghai's French quarter, where old Tsarist officers, converted into restaurateurs, knew so well how to ally the quality of their food with the melancholy of the steppes by way of their songs; nostalgic for the agreeable diplomatic life in China; nostalgic for the teeming streets and markets; nostalgic for the club where women were permitted to enter only once a year, and which possessed the longest bar—thirty meters—that I had ever seen.

Fortunately, our favorite Chinese friend, Chang Hsueh-liang, the man who had bought the three Italian planes, was on the ship carrying us away from China. He had decided to make the voyage to Europe, since two of his provinces—Manchuria and Jehol—had been taken over by the Japanese. With that ancient Chinese wisdom, he knew that it would be best to await better days by profiting from his immense fortune. And to better savor European life, by conserving a Chinese aroma, he had taken with him his personal advisor, his wife, his mistress, his children, and his doctor.

Since Chang, his wife, and his mistress were all three opium addicts, it had been difficult to prepare for the voyage. They had had to undergo detoxification. But after a first period of cure in a clinic, Chang had taken a villa to continue the cure. He had seen to it that two additional beds—one for his wife and the other for his concubine—were installed in his room. Though he was coming to Europe with us, he organized a farewell dinner for us. It took place in his room, and I must admit that it was most amusing to see him contemplating us while we ate, during which time he remained imprisoned in his bed, surrounded by his wife and his concubine, and had to content himself with watching the spectacle. What European would have had the wisdom and the sense of humor to organize such a banquet without being able to participate himself?

XI

Before he fell into disgrace and had his portfolio as Minister of Foreign Affairs withdrawn from him by Il Duce, Galeazzo Ciano was, as I have said, regarded by most of the Italian and foreign political personages as Mussolini's "heir."

Then, when the Rome-Berlin Axis began to show signs of leading to Italy's ruin, the opponents of Mussolini's Germanophile policy saw in Galeazzo Ciano the principal artisan of the alliance between Italy and Germany.

Finally, when Il Duce lost his power during the famous reunion of the Fascist Inner Council of July 24, 1943, and was arrested the following day by order of Marshal Badoglio, his successor as head of the government, the Fascist extremists considered Ciano a traitor who had plotted against his Duce and his benefactor. The rest thought of him as only one of the dignitaries of the regime, who had enjoyed the advantage over the others of also being Mussolini's son-in-law and had profited from that state of affairs by enriching himself and believing that one day he would succeed Il Duce.

However, at least according to his notebooks, Galeazzo Ciano had always been hostile to the Italo-German Alliance. Also, after Il Duce's arrest, Ciano's fate was determined by the very people with whom he had sided during the reunion of the Fascist Inner Council.

What had Galeazzo Ciano, the prodigal son of Fascism, the diplomat whose intelligence was denied by none, done to cut himself off successively from all sides and to place himself in a situation such that his only escape was a flight to Germany? And why the Germany of Adolf Hitler, whom he execrated?

How could a man who had been Mussolini's right-hand assistant for seven years, during hours that were crucial for Italy and the world, have committed such grave errors of judgment? Unless he had been merely a creature of Il Duce or of his own wife Edda, of whom the newspapers wrote that she was the most dangerous woman in Europe.

XII

Not only was I called a Messalina, but I was said to be
the Egeria of the regime. Well, I have always pitied those Egerias
reputed to have played a role in history.

Glancing through some newspapers recently, I suddenly realized how legends assume shape and fasten on to people. If those
papers were to be believed, it wasn't Hitler and Mussolini and
my husband who were the protagonists of what occurred between
1933 and 1945, but rather I, Edda Ciano. Thus, I discovered just
how celebrated I had been.

Just as my mother entered into history as a good woman with
an unfaithful husband, devoted to her wifely housekeeping duties,
submissive, and retiring—which was completely false—so I
was, from my marriage on, the person who led my father by the

nose, made a puppet of my husband, and built up, according to my own lights, the Italian empire.

Better still, my omnipotence did not stop at my country's frontiers, and even Adolf Hitler, succumbing to my charm and strong will, desired only to carry out my least desire. Finally, my power reached beyond the political field, and I intervened in all domains, even when it concerned going to Brazil to find the coffee that Italy needed for its *espressi* and its *capuccini*.

In a word, I was at one and the same time the Chinese Empress Tz'u Hsi, Catherine the Second of Russia, Catherine de Medici, Richelieu, Fouché, Queen Victoria, Mata Hari, et cetera.

In the July 5, 1939, issue of *Vu,* a French pictorial magazine, there was an article devoted to "The Seven of Present-Day Italy" and signed by Emmanuel d'Astier, which stated that Galeazzo Ciano, after having been appointed in 1936 as the youngest Foreign Minister in the world, began "his career as traveling salesman for Il Duce, a career in which he was essentially a puppet and Edda played the major role, as everyone knows." One of the photographs illustrating this article was accompanied by the following caption: ". . . Daughter of Il Duce, stern-faced and proud, she is followed by a circle of devotees and is the embodiment of ambition—to have her niche in history."

Another paper, *Paris-Soir Dimanche,* published on April 15, 1939, wrote on the first page, regarding the eventual appointment of my husband as Viceroy of Albania, that, according to the *Times* of the previous day, it was "Signora Edda Ciano, daughter of Mussolini, who persuaded her husband to accept the semi-crown of Viceroy so that, as his wife, she would take precedence over the Princess of Piedmont, born Marie-José of Belgium, wife of the heir to the throne, Umberto, at official ceremonies."

The December 8, 1938, issue of *Match* devoted four pages to my husband and, in the article accompanying the numerous photographs, I read on page 9: "In 1933, the Cianos returned to Italy. Edda, reunited with her father, exercised, as always, a profound influence over him. . . . Edda has not ceased to be the persevering inspirer of Italo-German rapprochement, acting through her husband and her father to achieve the Berlin-Rome axis, which is the personal handiwork of the Cianos."

The Sunday *Mirror* of July 30, 1939, sent to us by Italy's Consul General in New York, went even further. In an article entitled "Italy's Number One Woman," they wrote: "The most powerful wife in Europe today should be Donna Rachele Mussolini. But she isn't. Instead, she washes dishes on the cook's day off; minds her chickens in a hidden corner of the vast Villa Torlonia, where Il Duce makes his home. . . . The real First Lady of Italy is Edda Mussolini Ciano. . . . Edda Ciano is the only human being in the world who can talk back to Benito Mussolini."

Time of May 22, 1939, stated that Countess Ciano, who had made a voyage to Brazil supposedly for medical reasons, had in reality done so in order to buy coffee for the Italians, who were running out of it.

An Egyptian paper, *Al-Wafd al-Misri,* wrote on May 10, 1949, that Benito Mussolini asked only his daughter for advice.

Time even devoted its cover to me one week. What a boon to the ego!

Finally, according to the Egyptian magazine *Images* of February 16, 1942, I was neither more nor less than "the most dangerous woman in Europe." The article went on to say: "Edda rules her father with an iron hand. . . ."

Such an exposé of my occult power should flatter my ego and make me blush with pleasure and pride, even thirty years later. Only, it was simply not true, and the two persons to whose detriment I supposedly had exercised that power were the only beings whom I loved and admired with all my heart, and whom I still love today—my father and my husband.

It would be false to say that I was a poor submissive woman

who always remained in the background and whose sole ambition was to prepare delicious little dishes for her husband. But I was far from an Egeria, and this for two basic reasons.

First, like all Italian women, perfectly aware of my position as a woman—even though I had always regretted not being a man—I knew very well just how far I could go with impunity, and it would never have occurred to me to interfere in my father's or my husband's affairs.

Second, neither of them would have allowed me to encroach on his domain.

My father believed that a woman should remain a virgin until her marriage, then take care of the house, bear children, and, as I have said before, be willing to accept her husband's infidelity.

He had, it is true, higher ambitions than that for me, but he would never have thought of giving me the right to take the least initiative in political matters or in the direction of affairs of state, not because I wasn't capable of doing so but because I was merely a woman.

So he confined himself to asking me from time to time for my opinion about certain things or giving me precise political missions. It is some of the latter which were at the basis of that grossly exaggerated legend about me. But in all cases I was only a soldier faithfully executing orders within a well-defined limit. I never took the initiative with my father because I did not want to do so and also because he would have quickly put me in my place if I had done so.

Thus, even though I sometimes stood up to him, always with the greatest respect, Benito Mussolini, my father, was never my "property" and I never "ran him with an iron hand."

As to my husband, he was even more categorical about women than my father. To his mind, politics was strictly a man's affair. This does not mean that we did not ever have violent arguments when we discussed politics and were in disagreement, notably on the subject of Germany and the war. Galeazzo was hostile to both, while I was extremely bellicose and Germanophile.

Those discussions, moreover, almost always ended with my husband concluding, "In any case, you don't understand a thing!" And it would stop there.

On May 9, 1940, for example, I visited his office in the Palazzo Chigi before taking the train to Florence, where I was to attend the "Florentine May" celebration. I had gone to see him to protest the nonbelligerence of Italy and to manifest my shame at seeing our country, Germany's ally, refuse to stand by her side in the war. Galeazzo listened to my tirade with an ironic smile; then, when I had finished, he merely said, "You understand nothing. You would do well to get along to Florence. It is better that you interest yourself in music. . . ." A month later, Italy entered the war, but I must emphasize that, though I was delighted by my father's decision, I had absolutely nothing to do with it.

However, submissive or not to the will of my father and of my husband, I was, after all, Mussolini's daughter and the wife of the Italian Foreign Minister. Therefore, whenever I traveled abroad, even though it was a private and personal journey, I was treated with special consideration, which did not at all displease me. Also, even my purely social contacts with political personalities had repercussions at the Palazzo Venezia and the Palazzo Chigi.

For example, certain statesmen would seize upon such an occasion to transmit a message or a point of view to Il Duce, as was the case with Hitler, who desired to create a climate propitious to a rapprochement between Italy and Germany. Sometimes it was my father and my husband who would entrust me with a specific mission to sound out a situation or communicate a decision arrived at by the Italian government. Such was the case in 1934, at the time of a trip I took to London.

Before my departure my father had summoned me and, as though I were a military person leaving on a mission, he had given me very precise directives.

"During your trip," he said to me, "I want you to inform

any English whom you might run into—from the Prime Minister to the lowliest officer of the Guard—that we Italians have decided to march on Ethiopia. And be sure to tell them that our decision is irrevocable and cannot be reversed!"

Once I was in London, I did not hesitate to tell everyone about this irrevocable decision: "We will take Ethiopia, whatever you may think about it and despite what you decide to do!" As perfect Englishmen, my companions received the news with absolute phlegm, whether they were personally in favor of it or not.

The only two persons who had a distinct reaction were Lord Rothermere, the owner of the *Daily Mail,* and Mr. James Ramsay MacDonald, the British Prime Minister.

"Very well, very well! Go and handle those destitute blacks," the press lord told me, during a lunch at Noel Coward's home. "What is all this fuss about intervening in other countries? Don't worry! We ourselves created an empire, after all!"

Ramsay MacDonald, on the other hand, had the reverse reaction, although expressed in an extremely diplomatic fashion. It occurred at the House of Commons. Mr. MacDonald listened to me attentively; then, crossing and uncrossing his legs, he replied, "Very well, but I suppose you have considered seriously what the consequences of such an act will be?"

He then explained to me at length all the possible consequences that might ensue.

I replied, "Agreed. But are you going to declare war on us?"
"No!"
"So . . . !"

After that we went out to the terrace to have our tea.

At the end of about a month, my mission fulfilled, I returned to Rome and reported to my two chiefs—my father and my husband.

That trip to London was the only one made with specific instructions. Most of the others involved only general directives from my father or Galeazzo. "Go there, speak with so-and-so, meet this one, behave in such a fashion with that one," et cetera.

Even when I served as a sort of link between my father and Hitler, the only special instruction I received was to be careful of Rhine wine and its effects.

Before speaking about that I would like to emphasize one point, so that it may not be said that I accomplished secret missions for my father without my husband, the Foreign Minister, being informed. My father gave me directives, but they were not secret. He had either talked them over with my husband beforehand, or he gave them to me in his presence. In any case, Galeazzo always knew about them. And sometimes it was even my husband who transmitted my father's instructions to me.

To return to that memorable journey to Germany, which was the first step in the Italo-German rapprochement, I must admit that, at my departure, nothing of what later happened had been foreseen. At the start it was simply a tourist trip that I was taking at the invitation of my sister-in-law, who had married Count Massimo Magistrati, First Counselor at our embassy in Berlin.

I took the train alone and spoke to no one during the entire trip, since the train was occupied only by Germans and I spoke not a word of that language. That recalled to me a period in my childhood when my father would take me with him, but would tell me not to open my mouth or say my name, for around 1920 the name Mussolini was not very popular.

At first, since my first visit was unofficial, no particular attention was paid to me. With the assistance of my sister-in-law, my brother-in-law, and our Ambassador to Germany, Bernardo Attolico, I saw the sights and met different personages in the German government, notably Frank, Goebbels, and Goering, at the various dinners and receptions I attended.

Then on June 9, 1936, my husband telephoned to me in Berlin to say that he had just been appointed Minister of Foreign Affairs. This unexpected news immediately reached the German government and, from that moment on, my visit took on a completely different dimension and became official.

Everything changed. I was treated as the wife of the Italian Foreign Minister and given special consideration, similar to that reserved for us by protocol in my country, but with the addition of that solemnity and ponderous seriousness that is so much a part of German nature. And I must say that it is always enjoyable to be treated thus, even when one is used to it.

That is when I met Adolf Hitler. We were introduced at Lake Wannsee, at a tea hosted by the Goebbels, during which we took a charming boat trip together.

XIII

My first encounter with Hitler was not particularly thrilling, for it was not the first time that I had been received by a head of state.

During my trip to London in 1934, which had preceded the one I made under orders from my father to declare our firm intention to conquer Ethiopia, I had been presented to the British sovereigns. My curtsey was perfect, and I did not stumble.

I had been struck by the court dress, *"à la française"* I believe, with the tightly fitting trousers reaching to the calf and lace at the wrists and neck, worn by some of the ambassadors with great distinction, among them Dino Grandi, our representative to London at that time. It was also during that reception that the United States Ambassador, Joseph Kennedy, made a sensation by wearing plain clothes.

Then I was invited to attend the races at Ascot in the Royal Enclosure. Habituated to the strict etiquette of the Italian Court, I was astonished when King George V came up to me, opened his cigarette case, offered me one, and lit it for me.

Thus, my meeting with Hitler seemed to me a gesture of courtesy toward the daughter of Mussolini, and nothing more. I did not expect that it would turn out to have important consequences for Italy and serve as a link between the Führer and my father, the first step in a rapprochement that was to become the Italo-German Alliance, the Rome-Berlin Axis.

As a matter of fact, Hitler, who had not seen my father since 1934, during a rather disastrous trip that Mussolini took to Venice, wished to establish close relations with Il Duce, whom he considered to be his master.

My father had not been drawn to him in 1934. In fact, their conversations had left him with a definitely disagreeable impression. Later the assassination of Roehm and the bloodbath that had marked the "Night of the Long Knives," during which the S.A. leaders and the Führer's first collaborators were massacred with his full accord, had only served to confirm my father's first impression.

"Look," he had said to my mother, showing her the headlines in the paper announcing the bloody purge, "he makes me think of Attila. Those men that he has just killed are the same who helped him come to power."

The assassination of the Austrian Chancellor, Engelbert Dollfuss, on July 25, 1934, had only accentuated Mussolini's aversion to the Führer, for he knew that it had been the work of the latter's henchmen. And if France and England, our allies at that time, had listened to Mussolini perhaps there would have been no Third Reich.

However, since that time Hitler had undertaken a long and patient conquest of world opinion, to capture his opponents' esteem.

During the Ethiopian war he became the sole head of state

to refuse officially to carry out the sanctions adopted by the League of Nations against Italy. Therefore, despite those sanctions, we were able to receive the raw materials our country so desperately needed.

Given my Germanophile sympathies, I was, without being aware of it, the link between the Führer and my father. I found it normal that two dictators should be allies. And this all the more so since, as soon as he took power in 1933, I had begun to consider Hitler a veritable hero.

This was not due to a political point of view, but simply because I found the adventure of this man admirable as he stood up against all the great victorious powers of the First World War. I remember that I was in China when I learned of his nomination as German Chancellor. At that time I cried, "How wonderful that Hitler has been named Chancellor!" And Galeazzo exclaimed, "My God, it's a catastrophe!"

I continued to view with pleasure the economic and military successes of the new Germany.

XIV

Thus, as you can see, I was more than favorably disposed toward Hitler upon my arrival in Berlin. Nevertheless, my meeting with the Führer was most astonishing.

First of all, instead of a solemn conversation at the Chancellery, we enjoyed a simple, cordial talk, without the least sign of protocol, at the tea offered by the Goebbels on the shores of Lake Wannsee. The Goebbels' children were there too, and I was surprised to see Hitler play with them, giving all signs of pleasure at doing so and at hearing them call him "uncle."

To top off the day, we had a long boat trip on the lake, with Hitler by my side serving as a charming, eloquent guide.

I was really taken aback by such simplicity, which far surpassed that of us Italians despite our good nature and free-and-easy manners. If Hitler had had a daughter who had visited us in Italy as

I did in Germany, I am certain that my father would never have had the fantastic idea of offering her tea or taking her on a boat trip with him.

Even Frau Dollfuss, the only person whom my father might have treated in such a fashion, given the inexplicable as well as exceptional friendship between her husband and my father, had never been invited to dine with my parents, even when the Mussolinis and the Dollfusses spent their vacations together at Riccione.

My second and greater surprise concerned Adolf Hitler the man.

According to my remembrance of him during his visit to Italy in 1934, from the photographs I saw of him and the films that showed him haranguing the crowds or passing troops in review, the Führer had resembled a marionette with abrupt gestures and raucous voice, which made him seem slightly ridiculous.

However, when I stood before him for the first time, my impression was completely different. From the physical point of view, Hitler was no longer the timid, awkward man who had visited Venice two years earlier, wearing a shapeless hat and a too-large raincoat reaching to his ankles.

In 1936 he was dressed with a certain elegance; he was more self-assured and behaved like an amiable and cultivated man of the world. His blue eyes were charming, although I did not sense the hypnotic power they were said to possess. His voice was low and agreeable, less warm than my father's and not particularly beautiful, but it could be listened to with pleasure. He spoke calmly, listened attentively, and had a pleasant sense of humor. Even his Chaplinesque moustache, which had once seemed so amusing, now fitted his face and gave it a certain personality of its own.

I do not remember exactly what we said to each other that day, but I imagine that we spoke of the touristic beauties of Germany and Italy. The Führer did advise me about certain cities that he thought I should visit for their artistic riches, I seem to recall. I am sure that he asked me for news of my father and sent him his best regards. In short, nothing much of any importance was said, and in any case my memory does not serve me well. But then I did not know that our conversation was to have such an importance for the destiny of Italy.

During the years that followed I met the Führer on several occasions, and, whether it was at the Chancellery or at his headquarters in East Prussia, the "Wolf's Lair," I was always struck by his extraordinary kindness and affection toward me as well as by his patience.

For example, in 1942, when he learned that I wanted to visit the Russian Front, he tried first to dissuade me, then demanded that I be given shots by his personal doctor against all imaginable diseases. And again in 1942, during a visit that I made to a camp of Italian workers, I noticed that one of them had been badly beaten by a brutal German overseer. I went to see Hitler immediately afterward and spoke to him about the man, telling him that it was inadmissible to treat in this way men from a friendly nation who had come to replace the German workers who were off fighting.

The Führer flew into a rage, summoned those in charge of the services concerned, demanded that an inquiry be opened and ordered that those responsible for such brutality be arrested.

At the end of August, 1943, when we left for Spain aboard a German plane and found ourselves in Germany instead, Hitler invited me to his headquarters in East Prussia as soon as he learned that we had arrived.

Hitler awaited me at the door of his forest home. He held my hands in his, his eyes filled with tears, and he took me into his salon, where we were served some tea.

"Why did your father convene the Inner Council? What a terrible error he made!"

Those were his first words to me, after the usual salutations.

"And what will happen to my father?" I asked.

"Never fear. He will be liberated. We still don't know where he is being kept prisoner, but we will know very soon. And then, I promise you, I will do everything in my power to rescue him.

You can be sure that I will bring him to you safe and sound."

Then he led me into another room to show me the complete works of Nietzsche lying on a table along with a magnificent album, its cover encrusted with precious stones, in which there was only one handwritten letter—the good wishes that the Führer had prepared for my father's sixtieth birthday. Il Duce's birthday had already occurred, since he should have celebrated it on July 29, 1943, but Hitler was waiting to find out where he was imprisoned so as to send the gift to him. Which he did, moreover, several days later.

The next day he came to wish me a happy birthday, entering his personal train that he had put at my disposal (and my brother Vittorio's), carrying a bouquet of orchids that he had found goodness knows where.

We spoke of many things, and even though I sometimes made him angry, he never made a terrible scene with me or reproached me too severely. He explained to me that the Axis forces would definitely win this war, just as Frederick II of Prussia had won the Seven Years' War in spite of the coalition fighting against him.

I simply replied, "Yes, that's true, but in Frederick the Second's time there were neither Mosquitoes nor Americans. And then Churchill and Stalin are extremely clever. Believe me, the war is already lost, and the only thing to do is to make a separate peace with the Russians!"

Hitler leaped to his feet. "Nein! Nein!" he cried. "Anything but that! I shall never negotiate with the Russians, madam. You cannot marry water with fire. Peace with them is impossible!"

Hundreds of men had been executed, accused of defeatism, for much less than that. The Nazi dignitaries who were present, among them Ribbentrop and Himmler, and even my brother Vittorio, were terribly upset. I think that if they could have made me disappear, they would have done so with pleasure. But I was Mussolini's daughter and, even though a prisoner, he was still alive and remained the Führer's friend. So there was no question of harming a hair of my head.

"I don't think you have increased your chances of going with Galeazzo and your children to Spain, after such remarks," Vittorio commented ironically when Hitler had left. "You aren't much of a diplomat, my dear sister!"

Why didn't the Führer become much angrier than he did?

Because he loved frankness, plain speaking being a rarity; surrounded as he was by the constant *"Jawohl, mein Führer"* of his collaborators. Perhaps also because, even though I expressed ideas contrary to his, he knew that he could have confidence in my honesty, in my fidelity and in my friendly feelings toward his regime.

Whereas Galeazzo always considered his trips to Germany as irksome duties, preferring as he did Paris and the south of France —which he was not able to visit very often—I was delighted each time that I made the trip from Rome to Berlin.

I was pleased not only to meet some of the leaders of the Reich and get to know them rather well, but also to see how the Germans held out against the intense Allied bombardments.

The Nazi leaders and German high society in general lived just like their counterparts in all the European countries, at least before the war. Perhaps there was also something slightly more grandiose, more impressively solemn in their way of life.

Fashion headquarters was still Paris, for perfumes as well as for clothes. Moreover, like most Germans, Hitler had the complexes of a provincial with regard to Paris. He dreamed of going there, believing it to be something quite special.

As soon as Paris fell to the German troops Hitler hastened to make a visit, contemplating the marvelous monuments with admiration and forever praising the city, even transferring to Paris the ashes of the Duke of Reichstadt after having communed at Napoleon the First's tomb. He was so in awe of the city that he considered the conquest of France and its territories as completed once Paris had been taken, and he remained deaf to all of Mussolini's exhortations when the latter insisted that all of France and its overseas territories should be occupied by the Axis troops and that no free zone should be permitted.

My father believed, in fact, that those regions would become a base and a reservoir of men for a new French army. He was absolutely right, but he could never convince Hitler of that.

As I have said, social life in Germany was quite normal. They played cards and received a great deal. Evening dress was often worn. The receptions were extremely handsome, and the Führer often attended them or gave them himself, either at the Chancellery in Berlin or at his residence in Berchtesgaden.

He received his guests himself and always had a friendly word for each of them. During the receptions at the Chancellery, I was often struck by the number of very beautiful women surrounding Hitler. For the most part they were famous artists or women belonging to the highest social circles, and I never had the impression that the Führer was bothered by their presence at his side; on the contrary . . .

One day a Nazi dignitary pointed out one of these women to me. She was a marvelously beautiful blonde with the body of a goddess, and he whispered in my ear that for the moment she had captured the Führer's heart. It was not Eva Braun, whom I personally never did meet. This confirmed my impression that Hitler's misogyny and his "marriage with Germany" were only a legend.

Among the dignitaries of the Reich whom Galeazzo and I knew best, and with whose families above all I had the closest personal relations, were Joseph Goebbels and Hermann Goering.

If Goering was the most colorful man in the regime, Goebbels was, according to my husband, a "truly astute fox." And I myself would say that Goebbels was the greatest Minister of Information and Propaganda of all time.

Despite his puny aspect, his short stature, and clubfoot, Goebbels was a captivating man because of the intelligence shining in his brilliant eyes. Gifted with an extraordinary power of persuasion and seduction, to which were added his immense talents as an actor, Goebbels not only succeeded in creating the huge Ministry of Propaganda, but he was also the first statesman of the twentieth century to have convinced the masses as he wished by means of the radio, using nothing but his voice to reach their hearts and minds.

In private life, although blessed with a lovely wife and six children, the Reich's Minister of Propaganda was famous for the number of his female conquests, despite his physique. Few women could resist him, especially in the artistic and literary milieus, where his power of seduction was augmented by his Ministerial position.

Goebbels was unswervingly faithful to the Führer until the end. Most of Hitler's collaborators whom we met adored him, but the nuances were different. Some of them, like Himmler and Goering, for example, envisaged, as everyone knows, following a political career after the fall of their Führer. But for Joseph Goebbels everything had begun with Hitler and would of necessity terminate with him. He never imagined that the formidable machinery he had set in motion could possibly serve anyone but Hitler, or that he, Goebbels, could live on after the fall of the regime established by the Führer.

He was, I believe, the most faithful man I met in the Third Reich. His fidelity was complete and he had no illusions about the consequences of a defeat, as I had the occasion to ascertain in 1942, three years before the fall of the Reich.

One evening, during a dinner party at the Goebbels', I was surprised when Magda Goebbels rejoined her husband and me in the salon and told me, "If the war should be lost, we will all kill ourselves, including the children. Death is better than the Russians. We believe in the Führer. If he disappears, we shall disappear with him."

She pronounced those words with great calm, speaking of the vials of cyanide she was holding in reserve as if their use were a

Edda Mussolini Ciano

Galeazzo Ciano

Second from the left, the young Galeazzo Ciano as a lycée (high school) student at Livorno in May, 1918, when his father made him dress in a sailor suit to prevent him from frequenting prostitutes. Wearing a straw hat, his friend Tito Torelli.

Villa Torlonia. Edda Mussolini before her marriage, with her father, her paternal uncle Arnaldo (to the right of Il Duce), her paternal aunt Edwige (behind Edda to the left), and Prince Torlonia (to the left of and behind Edwige).

Edda and Galeazzo Ciano on the day of their wedding, on the lawn of Villa Torlonia. After this first marriage in the family, Rachele Mussolini swore that when the other children wed the receptions would be given in a hotel.

At winter sports in Terminillo, Benito Mussolini (behind and to the left), Donna Rachele, his wife (in front, wearing a white sweater). The person to the right, with a moustache, is Costanzo Ciano, Edda's father-in-law. Terminillo was discovered and expanded as a ski resort by Mussolini.

One of Rachele Mussolini's rare letters to her daughter Edda after the assassination attempt on Il Duce in 1926.

Dearest Edda,

I have received your letter and hurry to answer as I have always done. Thank God, Papa is well and no longer must wear a bandage on his nose. My birthday is over and Papa remembered it. He sent me a telegram from his ship en route to Tripoli.

I thank God every day for having saved his life and I shall continue to pray to Him to protect Papa from danger.

The masons have just about finished messing around here . . . and the garden is planted and looks lovely.

– Work hard, little one, and don't fall and hurt your head again. Many kisses.

Your mama.
Vittorio and Bruno send many kisses.

Il Duce's wound was caused by Violet Gibson, an Englishwoman who shot him in 1926 in Rome.

Signora Mussolini never went to grammar school; she taught herself to read and write.

Edda Ciano in China, invited on an expedition by the strong man in Chiang Kai-shek's government, Chang Hsüeh-liang. Galeazzo Ciano's wife used her charm to obtain an order for planes for the Italian government which had been destined for the French.

Galeazzo Ciano in the first months of serving as Minister of Foreign Affairs. Shortly before falling from power, he complained to a friend about working like a cart horse while Fascist dignitaries weren't working at all.

One of the rare photos of the Ciano family on the beach
at Viareggio. Edda Ciano disliked not being able to relax
without immediately seeing hordes of people crowding
around her. Mussolini also feared a crowd ever since the
day when, having "shed" his personal guards in Rome, he
was crushed by the crowd of Italians on the Via Nazionale.

Ironic sight: Galeazzo Ciano with his arm around the shoulders of one of his best friends, Allessandro Pavolini. Several years later, Pavolini demanded and obtained his head.

Edda Ciano, nurse during World War II. Beside her, Padre Pancino, one of her most faithful friends.

Edda Ciano as a nurse during an official ceremony at Tirana, Albania, in the company of Marshal Cavallero. Discipline was extremely rigid, and the fact that she was Il Duce's daughter changed nothing.

Photograph taken by Heinrich Himmler's services when the Cianos were supposedly to be taken to Spain.

Original of the *Ausweis* delivered by the Gestapo to Edda Ciano to allow her to return to Italy from Germany in 1943. The *laissez-passer* was in the name of Emilia Santos and not Emma Santos as certain historians have affirmed.

CD 14075

REFERENCE CARD

rpt February 1, 1943

ITALY

CIANO

He, BADOGLIO, GRANDI, CABALLERO, and UMBERTO, according to a report, are now persuaded that the defeat of Italy is inevitable; being faced with the loss of power and holdings, they probably are susceptible to promises of future protection and hints that they might hold power; it is possible that such a group could deliver a part of the Navy and the Army.

CD 20158

C

ITALY

rpt June 21, 1943

CIANO

Mussolini stands for a fight to the finish, but Ciano, PAVOLINI, and GRANDI do not share this view and they remain in the background.

Reports from the Intelligence Service concerning Galeazzo Ciano (in English).

-781

NN

REFERENCE CARD

ITALY

Ciano

Ciano is the most hated man in Italy; is now a super-millionaire and considering he was broke a few years ago the people are wondering just where all their contributions to the Fascist Party are going.

One of the last photos of Mussolini, several weeks before his death, during the Italian Social Republic.

TELEGRAMMA IN ARRIVO	Decifrato da
N. d'ordine 1849	Cap.Brandi

Partito 19.6.37 XV *ore* 20.17
Ricevuto 19.6.37 XV *ore* 21.00

Decifrato ore 21.30

F.M.J.

Per S.E. BENITO MUSSOLINI Capo del Governo
Italiano.

Nel momento in cui le truppe nazionali entrano
vittoriose in Bilbao , Le invio insieme al mio
il saluto più entusiastico di questo esercito
orgoglioso di avere corrisposto alla fiducia in
lui riposta da codesto gran Popolo e dal Suo
Duce , pregandoLa , nel dare a S.M. l'Imperato-
re notizia di tale successo , di esternarGli
i migliori sentimenti del popolo spagnolo e
del Generalissimo Franco .

Generalissimo Franco

Telegram sent in secret from General Franco to Mussolini on June 19, 1937.

For His Excellency Benito Mussolini, Head of the Italian Government.

As our national troops enter victoriously into Bilbao, I send you my greetings and that of this army, proud of having been worthy of the confidence that this great people and its Duce have placed in it, asking you to transmit to His Majesty the Emperor the news of this success and to send him best regards from the Spanish people and from General Franco.

GENERAL FRANCO

Handwritten letter from Cardinal Maglione, Secretary of State at the Vatican, to Galeazzo Ciano. At the same moment that this letter arrived, Ciano was asking the Holy See for right of sanctuary for himself and his family. According to Edda Ciano, the answer was negative.

Excellency,

I ask you to excuse me for replying only after several days of delay to your kind letter of the first of this month. I was waiting for several moments of liberty to write . . . [unreadable] . . . I feel myself obliged to do it.

I have passed on to our Sainted Father the expression of your noble, filial sentiments for which His Holiness thanks you with all his heart and sends you his paternal best wishes and his benediction.

As to me, I must tell you, Excellency, that it is not without . . . [unreadable] . . . that I keep close to my heart the immutable memory of our meeting, that . . . [unreadable] . . . Your Excellency procured for me. I will accompany you with my good wishes and my prayers. [End unreadable]

19 novembre 1943=XXII

RISERVATA=PERSONALE

Eccellenza
la Contessa Edda Ciano Mussolini
                    S E D E

    Gentile Contessa,

    il DUCE mi incarica di farvi recapitare l'acclu
sa Sua lettera.

    Vi prega di far sorvegliare attentamente i bam-
bini chè, dato il periodo eccezionale, potrebbero es-
sere esposti ad eventuali atti ostili.

    Vi prego, Gentile Contessa, di accogliere i sen
si della mia personale devozione

(Giovanni Dolfin)

Letter addressed by Mussolini's personal secretary to Edda Ciano to warn her against the dangers her children might be facing. Galeazzo Ciano was in prison in Verona at this time.

Her Excellence, Countess Edda Ciano Mussolini

Countess,

Il Duce has told me to deliver to you the following message.
He begs you to attentively watch over your children who, because of the exceptionally extraordinary period we are going through, could eventually be exposed to hostile acts.
Please accept, dear Countess, my personal devotion.

GIOVANNI DOLFIN.

Letter from Mussolini to Edda Ciano after the execution of her husband. This handwritten document has rarely been seen.

Dear Edda,
From time to time I receive news of you through official channels. Often I think of you as well as of the dramatic events that have occurred in your existence and in mine. One day perhaps you will be more understanding, especially if we can talk alone together. I have nothing to tell you about myself. It isn't worth it. I am grateful to Padre Pancino who is making it possible for this to reach you. I have been attending to Carolina so that she may rejoin you.
I embrace you as in the past.

Your papa

CAMPO DI CONCENTRAMENTO PER INTERNATI
LIPARI

Lipari, li

N° 3 di matricola

L'anno millenovecentoquarantasei il giorno 3 del mese di aprile,dinanzi
a Noi LACQUANITI Dr.Girolamo,Commissario Agg.di P.S.e Direttore della Co=
lonia di Lipari è presente MUSSOLINI Edda vedova CIANO fu Benito e di
GUIDI Rachele,nata a Forlì il I° Settembre I9IO,alla quale viene da noi
consegnata,ai sensi dell'articolo 185 T.U.leggi di P.S.,la carta di per=
manenza con la quale le vengono imposti i seguenti obblighi,oltre quelli
di carattere generale contenuti nelle leggi e regolamenti dello Stato:
I°)- Tenere buona condotta e non dar luogo a sospetti;
2°)- Non rifiutare il lavoro che per il tramite della Direzione della Co=
      lonia possa venirle offerto;
3°)- Non prendere alloggio in locali diversi da quelli stabiliti dalla
      Direzione della Colonia;
4°)- Non rincasare la sera più tardi e non uscire il mattino più presto
      dell'ora stabilita dalla Direzione della Colonia;
5°)- Non tenere o portare armi proprie o altri strumenti atti ad offende=
      re;
6°)- Non frequentare osterie od altri esercizi pubblici;
7°)- Presentarsi,puntualmente all'ora della libera sortita,della ritira=
      ta e alle ore I2 di tutti i giorni nelle località stabilite per gli
      appelli ordinari;
8°)- Non oltrepassare la linea di demarcazione indicata da apposite ta=
      belle e,comunque,non uscire fuori del centro abitato;
9°)- Tenersi lontano dalle spiagge,porti o posti d'approdo;
I0°)- Non giuocare d'azzardo;
II°)- Non detenere danaro oltre il quantitativo stabilito dal Direttore
      della Colonia e non darne ad usura;
I2°)- Non vendere,barattare,pignorare effetti di vestiario od altro forni=
      ti dall'Amministrazione;
I3°)- Non esercitare il commercio senza il permesso del Direttore della
      Colonia;
I4°)- Non dar luogo a schiamazzi o provocare altri rumori fastidiosi du=
      rante le ore di riposo;
I5°)- Non imbrattare o altrimenti deteriorare i muri,i mobili,il vestiario
      e gli altri oggetti forniti dall'Amministrazione;
I6°)- Non discutere di politica nè fare propaganda politica in modo anche
      occulto;
I7°)- Non ricevere o ricevere corrispondenza o pacchi di qualsiasi genere
      se non per il tramite della Direzione della Colonia;
I8°)- Non trattenersi per le strade in gruppo di persone superiore a 4
      escluse quelle di età inferiore ai I4 anni;
I9°)- Prestare obbedienza a tutti gli ordini degli elementi della forza
      pubblica preposti alla sorveglianza,presentando poi se del caso re=
      clamo al Direttore della Colonia;

Certificate of internment for Edda Ciano at Lipari after she had been brought
from Switzerland by the American authorities and handed over to the Italian
government at the end of World War II. There are several interesting
points in this bulletin:

*Article 7, which stipulates that Edda Ciano must "punctually present herself
when she leaves and when she returns and at noon daily."*

Article 8, "not to leave the center of the town."

Article 9, "not to gamble."

Article 16, "not to discuss politics or to propagandize, even in private."

*Article 18, "never to join with more than 4 persons in the street if they are
over 14 years of age."*

normal eventuality, as if, for the Goebbels', no other life was possible save that governed by Hitler.

Magda Goebbels was thirty-five, pretty, and the mother of six children. I was shocked not only by the determination of the couple but also by hearing Frau Goebbels speak so calmly of doing away with her children. And in fact, when Hitler did commit suicide in his bunker, the Goebbels did away with themselves and their children exactly as Magda had declared they would.

Goering was a strange case. He was a sort of condottiere who had degenerated into an extravagant satrap, for not only was he a sensual pleasure seeker but extremely eccentric to boot.

For example, in his residence at Karinhall, it was clear to see that he was mad about gadgets. He adored pressing a button to bring forth a movie screen and start up a machine that would project a film produced by Metro-Goldwyn-Mayer.

His villa was immense, resembling a chateau, and he had turned it into a veritable museum with bibelots, strange objects, and the paintings he was collecting. Despite the fact that it was a bit showy, I must say that the villa was decorated and arranged in rather good taste.

It has been said that Goering stole his pictures wherever the German army passed and enriched his private collection by these thefts. Perhaps he did behave that way in France or other countries, but, as I mentioned earlier, I do know too that many possessors of paintings who knew about his "hobby" often offered to sell him pieces from their own collections, and Goering bought them willingly. Then, when the war was over, those same people rushed to recount that their pictures had been stolen by the Germans. In this way, they had been paid a lot of money and yet were able to get back their "possessions."

I realize that the above was not always the case and that more than once a crate containing private or public artistic riches ended up in the collection of a Nazi dignitary. But I am certain that Goering's collection did not come only from pillaging and that he did not make a habit of behaving like a bandit.

Hermann Goering's extravagance had no limit. He had gone beyond the ridiculous and had reached the sublime.

At Karinhall, for example, while I was having tea with Princess Mafalda of Hesse and her husband, I saw a superb lion come toward me, then stop by the table and take a biscuit in its mouth. Sometimes it would place its head gently on a guest's knees and lick its chops, much to the person's dismay.

Another peculiar idea of Goering's was to dress according to what kind of hunting he was going to do when he left on an expedition. For example, when he planned to hunt bison, he wore clothes identical to those of a fifteenth-century hunter. Then, if he were going to do something else later, he changed clothes and would be seen in a uniform like no other we had ever seen, especially designed for him in a material whose color oscillated between violet and rose. The color was original, to say the least, for a marshal, and on the uniform he wore a battery of swords, daggers, decorations, and multicolored ribbons. And he would, in fact, change his costume at the blink of an eye, as well as his rings and other trinkets, four or five times a day if not more.

In this connection, I recall an episode that caused much worry to my husband at the time. It occurred in May, 1939, during the signing of the Italo-German pact, and Galeazzo wrote of it in his notebooks.

My husband noted that when Goering saw the necklace of the Annunciation around Ribbentrop's neck—the highest Italian decoration, which made of its bearers the cousins of the King of Italy —his eyes filled with tears and he created a jealous scene with Mackensen, the German Ambassador to Rome. He told him that only he, Goering, deserved such a decoration, because he had been the only real promoter of the Italo-German Alliance.

Mackensen spoke to Galeazzo, who, thinking that it would be easy to procure it for Goering, promised to intervene with my father and with the King. It was always Il Duce who proposed to the King that a decoration or noble title be bestowed.

However, my husband had a great deal of trouble convincing

Victor Emmanuel III to give the decoration to Goering. The King had no respect for him and refused to change his mind. A year of bargaining was necessary, plus scenes made by Goering, and, finally, a conversation between my father and the King, before Goering finally received it.

Galeazzo wrote in his memoirs that my father said to the King, "Your Majesty, it is perhaps a bitter pill that you must swallow, but under the circumstances everything points to the sagacity of such a gesture."

We were only a month away from entering the war on the side of the Germans, it is true, but for the moment, because of our position as nonbelligerents, my father did not want to irritate the leaders of the Reich.

One might have thought that Goering's extravagant behavior would have finally rendered him disagreeable, annoying, even antipathetic. On the contrary, he was exceedingly likable. Despite his obesity, he was still a fine figure of a man, and his voice was extremely agreeable. I cannot explain why it was so, but he succeeded in inspiring friendly feelings in most people.

Even my father and Galeazzo, though they were difficult in their judgments of people, were both fond of Goering. I think they were charmed by him and also found him rather intelligent, And then, during the war, he was the sole figure to lighten the monotonous nature of the Germans with his eccentricities. In addition, it should not be forgotten that Goering had proved his courage and had been a truly valorous pilot during the First World War. And finally, when Hitler had suffered his first setbacks during his conquest of power, Goering was at his side and showed his mettle as a man of action. What sometimes seemed like mere eccentricity was in fact completely sensible, occasionally extremely judicious.

One day, for example, I had occasion to visit an immense room at Karinhall in which had been installed a magnificent electric train circuit. Nothing was lacking, and I was impressed by the stations, garages, bridges, tunnels, signal lights, and switching posts. I thought that it was merely one of those gadgets Hermann Goering so adored, especially since the toy seemed to amuse him enormously. So you can imagine my astonishment when he explained that it was a toy, but an extremely useful toy for Germany: It was the replica of all the secondary railway lines in Germany, and, in playing with it, the Reichsmarshal was studying their utilization in case of the destruction of the principal railway lines.

Each time that we spoke of the war he said to me, "We must do two things before all else: take over Malta and occupy England." And he added, "But above all, we must never, never open a Second Front to the east. That would be the ruin of us!" However, not only did the Axis forces take neither Malta nor England, but as soon as Europe was occupied, Hitler launched into that hazardous venture—the war with Russia—which turned into an absolute catastrophe. And this Goering had foreseen.

I don't know whether it is because he amused him or because he recalled to him his first battles for power that the Führer tolerated Goering. It is known that Hitler, who was sober and never playful, pardoned everything his marshal did and called him by his first name. Perhaps he appreciated his intelligence, his journalistic talents, his writing ability.

Galeazzo often had the occasion to meet with Himmler, and I myself met him several times. We knew that he was the head of the S.S., of the Gestapo, but we considered him no more than a government functionary. And nothing in his attitude could have been taken as a sign that he was the monster brought to light toward the end of the war. With his pince-nez, his timid attitude, his air of being a quiet, fatherly type, he resembled a schoolmaster rather than a man capable of accomplishing or ordering such crimes or a leader who wielded such power. Not only were Italians unaware of what he was really like, but I believe that very few Germans realized what Himmler really was before the end of the war.

As to Ribbentrop, an incident occurred between us in 1942.

Before making a trip to Russia I had wished to see the effects of the Allied bombardments on Germany, and, with a friend, Princess Giovanelli, I had decided to visit Lübeck, which had just been bombed, as well as Hamburg and Bremen.

However, we couldn't seem to succeed in leaving Berlin for those cities, since Ribbentrop was against our trip. He refused to help us and pretended each day that he was going to give a great luncheon in my honor.

Finally I had had enough of such nonsense. I stamped my foot and replied to the people in the Ministry of Foreign Affairs, "I am here to see those cities. If Herr von Ribbentrop wants to give a luncheon in my honor, he is welcome to do so, but it can wait until my return from Lübeck."

In the face of such an attitude, Ribbentrop could only comply with my wishes. He put a special train at our disposal, and Princess Giovanelli and I made our trip. On our return Hitler's Minister of Foreign Affairs organized the famous luncheon.

I even recall that the Japanese Ambassador to Berlin was there and became quite drunk. The Germans of some consequence who attended the luncheon did not turn a hair, but I think he was told later that he would be well advised to watch his conduct in the future.

Since he had given the luncheon after my most successful trip, I thought that my altercation with Ribbentrop had been forgotten. But I had misjudged the Foreign Minister.

My father and Galeazzo were in Germany, at Berchtesgaden, I believe, to meet with the Führer. Ribbentrop used the occasion to take revenge for my obstinacy and insolence. He explained to my husband that my caprices were beginning to make me frankly insupportable and that many people were becoming ill disposed toward me.

Galeazzo was most displeased by all this, not only because those observations were made by the man in the German government whom he least liked, but also because at that moment his relations with Berlin were tense enough without the additional strain caused by the incidents that I had provoked.

As I have said, I had wanted to make that trip to Lübeck to see the war "at firsthand." I behaved thus not because of masochism, for I had already experienced the effects of war. The very day that Italy entered the conflict against France and England, and only several hours after I had heard my father announce that Italy was fighting as an ally of Germany, I took the train for the hospital nearest the combat zone, Turin, where I wished to serve as a nurse.

I remember that I did not even say good-bye to my husband because I was in such a hurry to be useful and do something positive in the war that I had so clamored for. And, immediately upon my arrival in Turin, I had experienced my first aerial bombardment, carried out by French planes whose pilots did an excellent job. So I had known all about that aspect of the war since June 10, 1940. Also, as I noted earlier, in 1941, while I was a nurse on the hospital ship *Po,* it had been sunk by a British aerial attack. Thus I knew what it meant to find oneself in the sea, only saved from drowning by the grace of God.

But I had never seen a city and its inhabitants under a veritable rain of bombs. I wanted to live that experience, and, when I did, I was astonished at the stoicism and the discipline of the German people. When Princess Giovanelli asked the burgomaster who was showing us around how many bombardments Lübeck had suffered to be three-quarters destroyed, he replied, "Only one, but it lasted for two hours."

In that city reduced to smoking ashes, the inhabitants who had escaped death, just like the English when their towns were bombed, went about their occupations with amazing calm, cleared up the debris in the streets without the least panic and undertook to reorganize their life. It was marvelous to see such courage.

I am convinced that many of those reading these lines will be scandalized and accuse me of making an apology for Naziism.

Moreover, when I appeared on French television, as I have described earlier, I provoked quite a scandal and was accused by certain newspapers of having made an apology for Fascism because I had stated that I believed Fascism to be the best government Italy had ever had.

It is true that other French papers congratulated me for my courage, but I won't dwell on that. I want to point out that when I speak of the courage of the Germans or the benefits of Fascism, I am not being nostalgic. I am simply being honest and objective.

And I am being just as objective and sincere when I deplore the extermination of the Jews by the Germans. It is true that I believed that the Jews, although charming personally and in small numbers, represented a danger since they were eager for power and because at a certain period (and even today) they controlled the levers of command almost everywhere in the world. I was equally convinced, because the propaganda affirmed it and there was nothing to prove the contrary, that the Jews had neither pride nor a sense of humor, and I was delighted to be an Aryan.

But I shivered in horror when I learned what the Germans had done to them, for such extermination cannot be justified, and my father would have opposed it with all his force if he had known of it. I was sincere when I felt such horror and pity. Later I was also sincere when I stated my admiration for what the Jews had done in creating the State of Israel against the whole world.

When Rome experienced its first aerial bombardment, well after the other cities in Italy, my reaction was similar to that of many other Italians. Since great capitals like Warsaw and London had been bombed, I saw no reason why Rome should be spared.

Can I be accused of thus singing the glories of the Allied pilots and justifying the destruction they caused?

I know several people who admired Hitler, who drank more than once to the victory of his German army, who sympathized—

and sometimes even more—with certain leaders of the German Reich but who, once Germany was beaten to the ground, hurried to forget the recent past.

"Hitler, don't know him" is an expression that I have often heard in Germany, where people cannot seem to succeed in ridding themselves of their remorse at having brought such a man to power.

I myself prefer to say, "Hitler, Goering, Goebbels? I knew them." It is more honest.

XV

ONE DAY MY FATHER HAD SAID TO GALEAZZO, "WARS ARE NEC-
essary from time to time. They forge men's wills."

"Yes, but they also kill," my husband had replied.

An aspect of what set apart my husband from my father is indicated in this exchange: one admired force, the other feared it.

You must not think, however, that Mussolini was a thorough-going warmonger and that Ciano was an inveterate pacifist; the former more than once tried to save the peace when things were ready to explode, and he sometimes succeeded, while the latter supported military operations and territorial conquests in which he believed.

But the real point of divergence between my father and my husband, which began in 1940, involved the Italo-German Alliance, because of what Galeazzo felt were the dangers implicit in it for our country and his disagreement with the attitude of our German allies toward us. This whole subject is very intricate, because of the fact that my father was not a blind admirer of Hitler and the Nazi regime, while my husband was not an unbending opponent of the German leaders.

Moreover, at the outset, the divergence was due to their respective turns of mind, to a predisposition based on their intellectual formation, and to their natural sympathies.

At bottom, my husband had never liked Germany or the Germans, not for political reasons in the beginning, but simply because he was a true Latin and therefore not attracted to their mentality. The Germans were too Nordic for him, and he considered that they lacked a sense of humor (not always true), warmth, and levity. He felt much closer to the English, the Spanish, the Portuguese, and above all the French, whose language he spoke easily and well. He also enjoyed the Chinese, who, although not Latins, had manners and customs that he admired.

Well before the war he went to Germany reluctantly, even though his position as Foreign Minister and as Il Duce's son-in-law brought him an always perfect and sometimes warm reception from the leaders of the Reich. It was worse for him when the extension of the conflict and of international tension transformed these missions into austere reunions, with Hitler giving hours-long monologues and the German Ministers talking only of campaigns, losses, and gains, et cetera.

On the other hand, he enjoyed going to London and he much admired the English for their self-possession, their humor, and their elegance.

But it was in France that he felt at his best, almost at home. Everything about the French pleased him: their literature—with which he had been nourished at a very young age, their cooking, their shops, their way of speaking, their wit. And when he made an official trip, he always tried to stop in Paris if it was on the way, even for just a few hours of walking through the streets of the French capital. And, when possible, he would avoid the embassy and reside either at the Hotel Lotti or the Prince de Galles, so as to feel more Parisian!

I must admit that I neither understood nor shared that infatuation. The French were too Latin for me, too close to us Italians to be able to attract me. I preferred the English and I loved going to London.

My father loved Germany, for his part. Not so much Nazi Germany, which at the outset he had no reason to appreciate particularly, but that Germany which had given birth not only to men such as Wagner, Nietzsche, Kant, Goethe, Schiller, Luther, and even Marx, but also to great militarists like Frederick II and Bismarck. Everything relating to Germany interested my father, its poetry, its language, its customs, and even its old traditions. And he had a special admiration for the Prussian army.

One day, when the militia troops were preparing to parade, he explained to Galeazzo why he took such personal care of these preparations and attached such importance to the least detail, going so far as to spend hours observing the troops' movements, hidden behind the blue drapes covering the windows in his office. He told him that he believed in the efficacy of the Prussian methods and wanted to adopt them, since 1,400,000,000 men from several continents had been needed to vanquish 60,000,000 Germans rendered quasi-invincible thanks to the iron discipline and feeling of power inspired in them by the rigidity of their Prussian training.

But upon Hitler's attainment of power my father and my husband found themselves on the same wave length, with some variations, regarding the feelings inspired in them by the new master of Germany and his regime.

"What a catastrophe!" Galeazzo had said upon hearing the news. And yet, there was no question at that time of a possible war, nor of an eventual alliance between the two countries, nor of any shadow that could come between Germany and Italy. We were in the eleventh year of the Fascist regime, and my father's power was solidly anchored in all classes of Italian society.

"He is a violent human being, a man incapable of controlling himself, and he is more stubborn than intelligent," my father had said to my mother after his first meeting in Venice with the Führer in 1934. And, as I have said, that first impression was only strengthened by the liquidation of Roehm, et cetera.

Yet the fact that Hitler had restored order in Germany did not signify to my father nor to my husband that Italy was in any danger. But both were alarmed by the methods employed.

It was during the following years that the opinions and feelings of my father and of my husband began to diverge. But even then, that did not imply a rupture in their community of ideas, if only because it was my father who conducted Italy's foreign and domestic policies and my husband had to execute his orders, whether in agreement or not with him, or else leave the government.

When Hitler restored the economic position of Germany, developed its industry, and increased its military power, Galeazzo began to observe its progress with mistrust and apprehension. My father, on the other hand, looked upon it with increasing interest and admiration.

Certainly, the Führer's attitude in 1935–36 concerning the Abyssinian war, facilitated things. There was also the triumphal official tour that my father made in Germany in September, 1937, which gave him a more precise idea of the power of that country, the will of its chief, and the unity of its people behind their leader. Finally, in May, 1938, the Führer made another visit to Italy, this one crowned with success, and the two men became truly friendly.

Thus, on the human level, it is incontestable that my father felt much more esteem for Hitler than did my husband, just as it is certain that the personal relations between the two statesmen counted for 80 percent in the Italo-German rapprochement.

How did our two traditional allies—France and England, beside whom Italy had fought in the First World War—feel about this budding friendship between Italy and Germany?

England and its countrymen had been a disappointment to Mussolini. Although he had expressed his admiration for England more than once, he found the country disagreeable because of its eternal "pea soup," which he claimed penetrated even the clothes in his suitcases. Concerning His Majesty's citizens, my father, as he explained to Galeazzo during the Anglo-Italian meetings in Rome in January, 1939, considered that they were no longer "of the same quality as the celebrated Francis Drake or those formidable adventurers who created the British Empire. They are merely the worn-out descendants of a series of rich generations of ancestors," he had added.

And the fact that the English had not budged when he had alerted Europe to the dangers inherent in the Führer's behavior and his territorial ambitions had only served to convince him even more strongly that they were poor and untrustworthy allies.

He had nourished friendly, even affectionate feelings toward France for many years. As with my husband, several factors drew him to that country: the language first of all, since he spoke it perfectly and had taught it in Romagna after having completed his studies in Switzerland. Also, Napoleon was his idol. He possessed a bust of the Emperor, which had its place in the house, and collected all works on the First Empire. Aristide Briand was a favorite of his and he followed his advice for a time. He admired France in general because of its historical riches, its exciting development from 1789 until 1918, and its army, which he regarded as one of the most powerful in the world.

But since 1936 the relations between the Popular Front government of France and the Fascist government of Benito Mussolini had become less amicable than hitherto. Not only did the opponents of the Fascist regime find sanctuary in France, like Pietro Nenni, once a prison companion of my father's at Forli when they were both Socialists, but they also possessed great financial means and official support, making it possible for them to lead a fierce propaganda campaign against my father. This infuriated him, naturally. Finally, over the years of Socialist power in France, the

155

attacks against Mussolini in the press and in the street had become so numerous and so vicious that he had ended by disliking the French.

In January, 1939, during a conversation with Galeazzo, he said to him, speaking of the French and commenting on an article in *Europe Nouvelle* about his personal life, "They will be the first to bite the dust. Such insults can only be erased by cannon fire and bombs." Galeazzo noted this commentary in his notebooks without adding any observation of his own, but he too felt a bit more irritated each day by those skirmishes, which were all the more stupid in that each time they occurred they pushed my father a little closer into Hitler's arms and only reinforced the chances of an Italo-German Alliance.

Galeazzo had noted on January 5, 1939: "Besides, time moves on. The anti-Italian manifestations in France and in Tunis, the gesture of Daladier, who wanted to cut his throat with a Corsican dagger, the press that insults us have created a climate of hate toward France . . ."

And three weeks later, on January 31 of the same year, my husband added to his notes: "The Axis is becoming increasingly popular. The Germans are responsible for such a result, as well as the French with their policy composed of vulgar insults and barely disguised contempt . . ."

In short, if in 1939 the climate between the two countries had not been so poisoned, things might have turned out quite differently. But the incidents that occurred between the Italians and the French concerning Corsica, and the Italian nationals living in Tunisia, whom the French authorities wanted to transform into French nationals against their will, went from bad to worse. The more or less secret missions of men like M. Baudoin, sent by Daladier and Bonnet to sound out the Italian government, turned out badly as well. And M. François-Poncet, the French Ambassador to Rome, soon found all the doors in the Italian government closed to him by order of Il Duce.

It is true that François-Poncet had succeeded in concentrating on himself all of my father's fury by declaring to the Uruguayan Minister Plenipotentiary, who had immediately repeated it to my husband, that Mussolini was "completely decadent intellectually." He had also written a letter, which was intercepted by the Italian Secret Services, in which he compared the Germans to the Italians, affirming: "In Germany, I discussed matters with gentlemen; here, however, I am dealing with valets become masters . . ."

So it was perfectly comprehensible that in January, 1939, the relations between the head of the Italian government and the French Ambassador should have deteriorated to the point where, during a reception given in honor of Chamberlain in January of that year, my father publicly turned his back on François-Poncet, who was trying to pay his respects.

By this time, it was obvious that Mussolini and Ciano had identical points of view about France and England. There remained Germany.

My husband had not changed his mind about Germany, despite the fact that some of the men in the government of the Reich, like Frank, Goebbels, Himmler, and Goering, attracted him because of their talents as statesmen.

He continued to distrust the Führer. And I remember an episode in Germany that reveals his attitude. It occurred when Galeazzo, along with my father, was trying to safeguard peace in September of 1938 during the Munich conference.

While my husband was walking with Hitler in the park at Berchtesgaden, the Führer brought up two possible results of a conflict. "We must win the war and we will win it. If we should lose it, however, we would no longer have the least reason for living and I would be the first to kill myself."

At that point, Giovanni Ansaldo, the director of *Il Telegrafo,* my husband's newspaper, who had heard the Führer's remarks, whispered into Galeazzo's ear, "Why doesn't he do it right now?"

Given the circumstances, the remark was extremely witty, but also rather serious. The fact that Ansaldo had dared make it not only in the presence of Hitler, who fortunately either did not hear it or did not understand it, but in the ear of the Italian Foreign Minister and his own employer at the paper proved that he had understood what Galeazzo's true feelings were. Also, the pleasure with which my husband repeated the anecdote to me, and even to his friends, upon his return to Rome indicated that he still had no great sympathy for Hitler.

My father, on the other hand, struck by the economic and military strides that Germany had made and surprised by Hitler's increasing self-confidence, would have been happy to ally himself with that country if he had not been held back by Hitler's increasingly bellicose ardor.

For, remembering the First World War, my father was convinced that France and England represented a potential force of arms with which they would have to reckon sooner or later. And he felt this way despite the fact that France and England had not made a move in answer to the assassination of Dollfuss and the announcement of Germany's rearmament.

Also, the Abyssinian and Spanish campaigns had considerably weakened our army and our war industry. My father and my husband were both aware that they needed time to regain their lost strength.

But when Ribbentrop came in October, 1938, to ask that the Anti-Comintern pact, already uniting Italy and Germany, be transformed into a Treaty of Alliance, stating that such an accord would be only defensive and that his country did not envisage the least conflict before two or three years, because the German army and navy were underequipped, both my father and my husband changed their minds.

They believed that such a treaty would allow them not only to become allied with a powerful country, but also to safeguard peace in Europe by becoming Germany's ally and moderating its warlike temperament.

Also, as my husband noted on January 4, 1939, this accord did not affect the relations existing between Italy and its First World War allies, since, before entering the war on their side in

1915, our country had belonged to the Triple Alliance, including Austria and Germany, but had maintained cordial relations at the same time with France and England.

The treaty of alliance between Italy and Germany, that is to say, the Rome-Berlin Axis, was thus signed by Galeazzo on my father's behalf, based on the certitude that it was a defensive agreement only, excluding any idea of war before two or three years.

But my husband, having been in absolute agreement with my father, soon discovered the truth and resumed his previous distrust, as the Germans did not take long to reveal their true intentions.

After certain information was furnished by our Ambassador in Berlin, according to which Hitler was interested in the oil wells in Albania, Galeazzo reacted strongly and warned Mackensen, the German Ambassador to Rome, that the Italian government considered Albania the same as it did any region of Italy, and that any intervention by Germany in the domestic affairs of that country would inevitably provoke a hostile Italian reaction.

Moreover, from that day on my husband was determined to annex Albania.

There the matter rested, but on March 15, 1939, at three fifty-five in the morning, Emil Hacha, President of the Republic of Czechoslovakia, signed his country's capitulation, after a dramatic encounter with Hitler, "placing the future of the Czech people and territory in the hands of the Führer of the German Reich," according to the official communiqué. German troops invaded Bohemia, and Prince Philip of Hesse came to Mussolini to inform him of the operation—after it was all over.

This time my husband was convinced that the Germans were not as loyal to the Italians as they pretended to be and that only an accord with the great Western powers could save the peace. On March 19, 1939, he wrote in his notebooks:

"The events of these last days have completely changed my opinion about Hitler and Germany. He is disloyal and a traitor, and no policy can be planned in cooperation with him. I intend to try to persuade Il Duce to reach an accord with the Western powers also. But will they have the necessary minimum of good sense in Paris to make this possible, or will they once again compromise any possibility of agreement?"

My father was also extremely vexed by Hitler's attitude, but he hesitated to move. On the one hand, he did not want to forfeit an alliance with a strong country, Germany, whose leader professed to be his friend; on the other hand, he feared being duped, despite the fact that the Germans affirmed that they recognized the preeminence of Italian interests in Croatia and that they had no designs on the Mediterranean Sea.

But, as my husband noted at the time, my father was tormented above all by the need to abide by his promise to Hitler and to remain faithful to the friendship that Hitler had manifested toward Italy at the time of the "sanctions" in 1935. "We cannot change our policy because we are not whores . . ." Papa said to Galeazzo. And one evening, as he was contemplating a painting given to him by a Hungarian, at the bottom of which was written, "Treaties are not eternal," my mother heard him murmur, "Nevertheless, Italy must respect her agreements."

I think that in saying this he was thinking of the volte-face of our country in 1915, when we became the ally of France and England despite a treaty binding us to Austria and Germany. In his heart of hearts, my father, who had extolled that change in policy, had always felt a sort of remorse because of it.

Thus, in 1939, the points of view were as follows:

Mussolini hesitated because he doubted the loyalty of the Germans and feared a reaction from France and England, in whose power he believed, if he were to ally himself with Germany. But, on the other hand, he did not want a proletarian country like Italy to break its ties with another proletarian country, Germany.

As to Galeazzo Ciano, he was convinced that Italy would be committing an error and would be the loser for it if she allied herself with Germany, especially given the fact that he had no illusions as to the loyalty of the German leaders or their pacifism.

The question was this: Could Italy be Germany's ally without betraying her traditional friendship with France and England, and could she avoid participation in a war launched by Germany without violating obligations imposed by a treaty?

On August 9, 1939, my husband decided to go to Salzburg to meet with Ribbentrop. As he mentions in his notebooks, my father insisted that Galeazzo prove to the Germans, with documents in hand to back up his arguments, that "it would be mad to declare war at this time. Our preparations for war are not far enough advanced to assure us a definite victory. We could not hope for more than a 60 percent chance of success. On the other hand, three years from now the possibility would reach 80 percent." And Ciano added: "Mussolini still believes in his idea for an international conference. I think that would be a very good thing indeed."

Before leaving Rome on August tenth Galeazzo noted too: "Before leaving me, Il Duce told me again to insist on the necessity of avoiding a conflict with Poland because it would be impossible to limit such an adventure and a general outbreak of war would be disastrous for everyone. . . . I have strong misgivings about such an intervention."

After his first conversation with Ribbentrop at Salzburg my husband noted on August 11: "The Germans' will to fight is implacable. They reject any solution that might satisfy them and avoid a war . . ."

And before going in to dinner, my husband finally asked Ribbentrop, "Do you want Danzig?"

"More than that," was the reply. "We want war!"

Henceforth, everything was clear. Mussolini and Ciano tried to avoid Italy's being dragged into a conflict that might blaze out from one day to the next. But my father did not want to betray his promise of alliance with Germany, so he hesitated before taking any clear stand.

On August 10, while he was in Albania, my husband received a telegram from Anfuso, his principal private secretary at the Ministry, informing him that his presence in Rome during the

161

evening would be most advisable. He canceled the rest of his trip and returned immediately to Rome, where he was notified that my father wished to inform the Germans that he would be by their side if a conflict should occur. Galeazzo succeeded in holding off the dispatch of this message until the next day, so as to attempt to intervene with my father, as the English had asked him to do, and persuade him to attempt to settle the Polish question peacefully.

And on August 21 my husband spoke to my father. "Il Duce," he said, "you must not march beside the Germans. My unswerving loyalty to you gives me the right to speak my mind. I went to Salzburg in order to try to establish a common position, and I found myself facing a *diktat*. It is the Germans and not we Italians who have betrayed the alliance in which we were to be their associates and not their slaves. Tear up the pact, throw it in Hitler's face, and Europe will proclaim you the leader of the anti-Germanic crusade. Do you want me to go to Salzburg? I will do it, if you so request, and I will know how to talk to the Germans. Hitler will not make me put out the cigarette as he did with Schuschnigg!"

He succeeded in obtaining from my father agreement to send a memorandum made up of four points, of which he felt only one to be important—that Italy would not intervene in a conflict provoked by an attack against Poland. My husband also succeeded in wrenching from my father his agreement to set up an immediate rendezvous with Ribbentrop so as to discuss this memorandum.

He phoned to Ribbentrop from Il Duce's office, but he was difficult to reach. "Finally," Galeazzo remarked in his notes, "at 7:30 I was able to speak to him and I told him that I must see him at Brenner. He replied that he could not give me an immediate answer because he was awaiting an important message from Moscow, and that he would telephone me during the evening."

Galeazzo told my father of this conversation and the latter, suspecting that something was afoot, asked him what Ribbentrop's

162

tone had sounded like and whether he had seemed to be in a good or bad humor.

On August 21 at 10:30 P.M. Ribbentrop called my husband and informed him that he would prefer to meet with him at Innsbruck rather than at the Brenner frontier, because he had to leave for Moscow, where he was to sign an agreement with the Soviets. Suddenly everything had changed and Galeazzo's trip, as well as the memorandum, had become useless, for, with this agreement, Hitler had guaranteed the nonintervention of Russia in case of an invasion of Poland by Germany. And the French and English plan to use the Soviets as a dissuasive barrier to the Führer's dreams of expansion had just been exploded.

France and England did not hesitate to declare that they would intervene against Germany if a conflict broke out. My father became bellicose once again and asked Pariani, the Undersecretary of State for War and Chief of Staff of the Army, about the state of the Italian armed forces. Pariani replied that the army was in excellent condition, and Galeazzo noted: "Pariani is a traitor and a liar."

Why did he make this judgment? Because, contrary to my father, my husband was skeptical about the Italian army, and basically that is why he fought so hard to keep Italy out of an armed conflict.

The situation became increasingly tense between August 21 and 25, and Ribbentrop spoke constantly of the "Polish provocations."

An example of Galeazzo Ciano's fight to save the peace can be found in the archives relating to the period between August 21 and September 3, 1939. They reveal that Ciano was the only person in Italy to fight to keep our country from immediately entering the war. And I will not go into his activities in Munich, earlier, where he saved the peace by working behind the scenes.

He fought against the generals, who, to be sure of being in my father's good graces, constantly told him that the army was well prepared for war, when that was untrue. He fought against me, as I was trying to persuade my father to stand by Germany's side as a military ally. And, finally, he stood up to Il Duce himself, and succeeded in convincing him to delay Italy's entry into the war.

Paradoxically, his best ally in this enterprise was Hitler himself. On August 25, at 2 P.M., Mackensen informed my husband that he had a message for Il Duce.

Here I shall digress for a moment to explain how Mussolini and Hitler maintained contact with each other. First there were direct conversations, that is to say, my father and the Führer would meet either in Germany or in Italy, or along the frontier between the two countries, such as at Brenner. There they would discuss matters alone, sometimes in the presence of an interpreter, sometimes without one, for my father, contrary to what has been recounted, spoke German and understood it perfectly. Most of the time, at least when he was Foreign Minister, my husband would accompany my father and later prepare a summary of what had been discussed, adding his own conclusions and suggestions.

Il Duce and the Führer communicated by letter when they did not meet, but more frequently by way of messages sent through their respective Ambassadors. Mackensen, the German Ambassador to Rome, and Attolico, then Alfieri, who succeeded him in Berlin, received the messages, either coded or uncoded, from their respective governments and transmitted them to Hitler or to my father via the Minister of Foreign Affairs, who was Ribbentrop in Germany and Ciano in Italy, until February 5, 1943. Sometimes it was Ministers making the journey from Rome to Berlin, or vice versa, who would carry the messages, or Prince Philip of Hesse, who was the Führer's "special courier." The normal contacts between the two governments were carried out by the Ministers depending on the departments concerned, but even in those cases a trip to settle a technical question always had a political repercussion and gave rise to an exchange of views that invariably became the subject of a memorandum to my father from my husband.

Let us return now to that message of the Führer's which Mackensen gave to my father on August 25, 1939. Galeazzo wrote in his notebooks an account of how it helped him in his efforts to keep Italy from entering the war at the side of the Germans: "The message was ambiguous and metaphysical, concluding with the statement that the Operation would soon begin and asking for 'Italian understanding' . . ."

My husband leaped on Hitler's expression "Italian understanding." He succeeded in convincing my father that he should write to Hitler, and he immediately drafted a message stating that Italy was not ready for war but would enter on the side of Germany if the latter would agree to furnish the armaments and raw materials that Italy needed.

Galeazzo found that the text did not entirely correspond to what he would have wished, but, as he himself wrote, "It is already something, the first step has been taken."

As soon as the message was finished, he telephoned to Attolico and asked him to transmit it immediately to the Führer. In this way, he hoped to keep my father from changing his mind.

This procedure was habitual with my husband, who understood his father-in-law very well, and he even used it in his own case when, on February 5, 1943, he was relieved from his duties as Foreign Minister: He immediately asked for the approval of the Holy See to his nomination as Ambassador to the Vatican, for he was afraid that my father, who had proposed that post to him, would change his mind.

My husband's intervention occurred in extremis, because Attolico informed him the same evening that, after having given my father's message to the Führer, he had come across General Keitel, who was entering Hitler's office just as he himself was leaving it. And, before he had left the antechamber, he had seen Keitel coming out and heard him shout to his aide-de-camp, "The order for troop movements must be withdrawn!"

Soon afterward, moreover, General Roatta, the Military Attaché to our embassy in Berlin, telephoned to announce that the mobilization and troop-movement orders scheduled for that night had been rescinded.

And at 9:00 P.M., still on August 25, Mackensen came to the house to pick up Galeazzo and accompany him to the Villa Torlonia, where they gave my father Hitler's response to his message. According to my husband, the tone was rather cold, but it did attain the desired end: Hitler asked that a list of the Italian government's needs be sent to him.

When they left the Villa Torlonia, Mackensen, who was hostile to a "military adventure," as my husband noted, advised him to establish an absolutely complete list, the implication being that the Führer would find it difficult to give complete satisfaction and would thus perhaps put off for as long as possible the launching of military operations against Poland.

The next day Berlin asked again for the list. At 10:00 A.M. my husband, the Chiefs of Staff of the three branches of the armed services and Benni, the Minister of Industry, met in my father's office at the Palazzo Venezia. In the antechamber Galeazzo reminded them of their responsibilities and insisted that they tell Il Duce the truth about the state of the Italian army and Italian industry. He even asked them, as he wrote in his notebooks, not to display their "habitual criminal optimism."

The list was drawn up, and mighty impressive it was. My father asked for immediate delivery of everything that Italy needed, which came to 170 million tons of industrial products and raw materials, which would have necessitated 17,000 trains for their transportation from Germany to Italy—obviously impossible.

What Galeazzo Ciano expected—and hoped for—came to pass: Hitler rapidly replied that he could only furnish iron, coal, wood, and a few antiaircraft batteries. He admitted that he could understand Italy's situation and proposed that we simply adopt a friendly attitude while he took care of beating France and England after having smashed Poland.

According to my husband, as soon as Mackensen had left, my father drew up his reply to Hitler. He expressed his regret at not being able to intervene. He also proposed a political solution that would permit the peace to be saved as it had been at Munich and, in addition, would not make it look as though he were abandoning Hitler and refusing to stand by him. It was a victory for my husband.

However, despite the fact that he had won Italy's neutrality, Galeazzo was not very happy. He was even sad, because he was the sole witness to my father's pangs of conscience, which he described in his notebooks: "Il Duce is truly upset. His military instinct and his sense of honor prompted him to take part in the combat; but reason has kept him from doing so. He is suffering terribly. On the military level, he has been badly served by his colleagues. Believing that peace would be eternal, they led him to foster grave illusions, and today he was forced to face up to harsh reality. It has been heartbreaking for Il Duce, but Italy has escaped a great catastrophe—which is lying in wait for the German people . . ."

On August 27 a new message arrived from the Führer in answer to my father. He requested three things: 1) that we not divulge our decision to remain neutral so long as it was not necessary to do so; 2) that Italy make military preparations so as to fool the French and the English, 3) that Italian workers be sent to Germany to replace those Germans in the countryside and the factories who had been mobilized.

Il Duce replied immediately that he accepted all these conditions and that he promised to reexamine what Italy's attitude should be after the first phase of the conflict. Galeazzo noted that he believed my father was content to "remain watching at the window." But I am not so sure about that. Certainly my father was aware of our country's lack of enough raw materials and industrial products, which made it difficult to contemplate entering immediately into an armed conflict. Also, since the Munich conference, he had really believed that war would not break out before 1942. He had even made the necessary arrangements, taking into account this date limit, for the construction of a veritable city at the gates of Rome, to celebrate with great display the twentieth birthday of Fascism.

However, from the beginning, he had never been against an armed conflict. On the contrary, he had two reasons for thinking it to be essential: 1) in his opinion, war strengthened the people of a nation; 2) a new victory by the Italian armed forces would give Italy the territories and respect that it had needed for many years, not so that it might enslave other peoples, but so that it would be convinced that it was no longer an underdeveloped country looked down upon throughout the world.

Thus, in August, 1939, the points of view of Mussolini and of Ciano converged as to the ends to be attained, that is to say the neutrality of Italy and, if possible, peace in Europe, but they diverged as to their motives. My father hoped to gain time so as to be better prepared to take part in a war; my husband wished Italy to remain aloof from an armed conflict at any price, because he had no illusions about the efficacy of our army or about the German army's chances for victory, and also because he did not like war. One day, for example, one of Goering's aides-de-camp told him that the Reichsmarshal loved only precious jewels and war, and he replied that those were two pleasures that cost very dearly.

In any case, what my husband took for a victory was, in fact, only a respite; my father had agreed to make a decision based on prudence and good sense, but at bottom he harbored a sort of remorse, for he was convinced that he had let Hitler down.

However, on August 27 my husband was able to consolidate his victory of the previous day, when the English sent the Italian government the text of some proposals made to them by Berlin, which corresponded more or less to an offer of an alliance. London was convinced that Rome was fully aware of these proposals, which was logical on their part since we were allies of the Germans, but, in reality, neither my father nor my husband had been informed of them.

168

My father was extremely hurt, especially since he had been so remorseful at having left Germany to fight alone and had felt that he had been lacking in loyalty toward Hitler. My husband was less affected by the behavior of the Germans. When Il Duce told him that the maneuver had been provoked by the Führer, who had feared that Mussolini would succeed in resolving the crisis peacefully, as at Munich, which would increase his prestige, Galeazzo answered that perhaps that had played some part in the matter, but that he believed the explanation to be much simpler—the Germans were traitors and liars. At that moment if France and England had known how to maneuver properly, they would probably have been able to deter Hitler by supporting Mussolini in his search for a peaceful solution, because, with all their blunders, the Germans had ended by irritating my father to such a point that he no longer wanted to speak of Italy's later intervention and declared that he would do what he thought best when the time came. But, as events have shown, that is not the way things turned out.

That evening, sitting in his office, my husband noted: "I had to fight very hard to convince Il Duce to act as he did. I must add that all those who only think of telling Il Duce what he wants to hear completely abandoned me in this enterprise. The truth is the last of their preoccupations. Starace [Secretary of the Fascist party], whose moral and intellectual stature leaves much to be desired, said that the Italian women are content that there may be a war because they will receive six lire per day and will no longer have to be bothered by having their husbands underfoot all the time. What a disgrace! The Italian people truly don't deserve such a vulgar insult.

"But I intend to continue to fight alone," my husband continued, "because I am certain that it is in a good cause. War today would be a catastrophe, given our present material and moral conditions. I want to avoid it, at any price."

On August 29 the situation was relatively calm, and Hitler even informed Attolico that he was ready to receive a Polish plenipotentiary, but he was skeptical, for the slightest incident would be enough to explode the powder keg. On the other hand, he was awaiting a reply from England to his propositions. Galeazzo did not hesitate to call Halifax, the British Minister of Foreign Affairs, to urge him not to break with Berlin.

But on August 30 and 31 the situation became critical once more, both in the international as well as in the purely Italian area.

With regard to Italy, respecting one of the three secret clauses of the neutrality agreements decided upon between Germany and Italy, my father had taken a certain number of measures: mobilization of the army, blackout, requisitions, curfew. These dispositions were taken only to deceive the French and the English, but they had two unexpected consequences: London and Paris, believing that we were really preparing to enter into war, considered taking the initiative in opening military operations against Italy; also, according to my husband, the Italian people were extremely worried, and Bocchini, Chief of the Police, even claimed that in case of a mass movement in favor of neutrality, the *carabinieri* and the police would side with the population.

With respect to the international state of affairs, at nine A.M. on August 31 Attolico telephoned to Galeazzo to tell him that, unless something unforeseen should occur, war would break out within several hours. Galeazzo rushed to the Palazzo Venezia and, in concordance with my father, telephoned to Lord Halifax to inform him that Il Duce would try to intervene with Hitler, but on condition that he be given the authority to offer him something of value in exchange—Danzig.

Instead of discussing matters with the Führer, François-Poncet, the French Ambassador to Rome, and Lord Halifax, as well as Percy Loraine, the British Ambassador to Rome, refused the Danzig idea but remained vague about making other proposals in its place.

My father made one other attempt: he proposed a conference for September 5 to discuss the clauses of the Treaty of Versailles with France and England. Both countries accepted the idea, one skeptically, the other enthusiastically. Galeazzo, who had always detested conferences, merely hoped that this proposal would deepen the possibility of a rift between Italy and Hitler.

But that same night, at 8:30 P.M., what my husband had feared came to pass. Faced with the war measures taken by Italy, London cut off its telephonic communications between our two countries. Galeazzo immediately informed my father, who was deeply shocked. In his notebooks, Galeazzo wrote:

"Il Duce declared, 'That means war!' And he told me that the next day he intended to inform the Inner Council that we would not participate in the conflict.

"I replied: 'Tomorrow will be too late. The English and the French might by that time have committed acts which will make such a declaration too difficult to sustain. I am going to summon Percy Loraine and I shall reveal our true intentions to him. If there is a scandal, I will be finished, but the situation will be saved.' "

My father approved Galeazzo's proposal. Percy Loraine was received at the Palazzo Chigi by my husband, who immediately informed him of the telephone cut-off. Then he declared to the Ambassador, "But how can you believe that we would ever start a war against you and France!"

"At that point, Percy Loraine was deeply moved," my husband recounts in his notes "His eyes shone. He took my hands in his and said: 'I have understood that for the past two weeks, and I so informed my government. However, the measures taken in Italy during these past few days had shaken my confidence. I am so happy to have seen you tonight.' He pressed my hands once more, then he left a happy man.

Galeazzo informed my father of this conversation. In the meantime Il Duce had ordered that the lights be lit all over Rome, so as to diminish the anxiety and misgivings caused by the military measures.

The stratagem had worked, but Hitler, and above all Ribbentrop, bore Ciano a grudge for having revealed the secret agreements, and they took their vengeance in 1943. But, for the moment, that is to say on September 1, 1939, at 5:35 A.M., Italy's sword was not lifted as the German troops attacked Poland.

But history was on the march, the rattling of sabers covered those voices speaking of peace, and Italy's last efforts turned out to be in vain.

And, as always, when he made his decision, my father was calm. As to my husband, he was almost happy. But for how long?

After all this how can it be affirmed that Galeazzo Ciano was a statesman without intellect, a mere puppet who only executed Mussolini's orders, and whose actions did not conform to his ideas?

Who, in Europe, in France, in England, fought as he did to save the peace? If he had left my father to his own devices, Italy would have entered the war on September 1, 1939. I don't know what would have happened as a result, but I am sure that there would have been more deaths on all sides!

Thus, I can state positively that until September, 1939, Ciano succeeded in carrying out the foreign policy that seemed to him to be the best for his country. When he considered that the Pact of Steel was good for Italy and could protect the peace he signed it; when he believed that our country was not ready to take part in an armed conflict he did everything possible to keep Italy out of it. And he accomplished what he set out to do.

What did he do later? That is easy to see, and even in this other phase of his political activity he was perfectly coherent with his own personal ideas. And this until the very end.

XVI

ONE DAY IN SEPTEMBER, 1941, GALEAZZO RECEIVED A VISIT from the Minister of the Hungarian Legation in Rome, Mr. Mariassy. During the conversation Mr. Mariassy asked my husband whether he believed that the Axis would win the war.

I don't know how Galeazzo evaded the question, but I do know that after Mr. Mariassy's departure from his office, he noted in his diary: "The new Hungarian Minister to Rome is the classic example of the boring, ceremonious, vacuous career diplomat. He wanted to discuss politics and began by asking me if I thought that the Axis would win the war! I wonder what answer he expected in wartime from the Italian Foreign Minister, whom he was meeting for the first time. What an idiot!"

In fact, Mr. Mariassy was an extremely pleasant man, and his question, although not very diplomatic, was not at all idiotic. But my husband's reaction was understandable because it is obvious that he could not tell a foreign diplomat, whom he had never seen before, that he did not believe in an Axis victory.

My husband's opinion fluctuated between September, 1939, and September, 1941. From his belief in certain defeat, in June, 1940, he passed to a reasonable hope in an Axis victory; then, after June, 1941, he became skeptical once again about defeating the Allies, a reaction reinforced by his distrust of and lack of confidence in the leaders of the German Reich.

When he met with Mr. Mariassy in September, 1941, it would be more correct to say that my husband "no longer believed" in an Axis victory, for he *had* believed in it for a certain space of time.

In order to follow this evolution in his thinking, we must go back to September 1, 1939, when the German forces entered into war and Italy decided to remain a nonbelligerent.

By the third of September the lightning advance of the German troops in Poland was confirmed. On September 8 Warsaw was occupied.

This had contrary effects on my husband and on my father. Neutrality weighed on my father, even though he became angry with the Germans from time to time because they did not keep us informed of their decisions until after the fact, as, for example, the division of Poland between Berlin and Moscow. He feared that Italy would be judged unfairly by the German people, and when, on September 10, he learned from Attolico that the expressions *betrayal* and *false friend* were beginning to circulate among the German masses, who were manifesting a growing hostility to Italy, he reacted violently and wanted to force Hitler to publish the telegram in which the Führer had accepted Italy's neutrality. He felt that there was no reason why that text, known throughout the world, should not be read by the German people.

Mussolini suffered under the burden of this situation. My husband was aware of this and redoubled his efforts to strengthen Italian neutrality. While my father thought that the war would not last very long, because of the smashing successes of the Wehrmacht, Galeazzo was convinced that the end was not at all in sight.

On September 3 he noted: "It is now possible to predict that a rapid conclusion to the conflict is believable, for how can France and England help the Poles? And when the Poles will have been liquidated, how can these two countries engage in a conflict whose object no longer exists? Il Duce thinks that peace is near and that there will be no military confrontation. But I do think there will be one, and I believe that it will be long, uncertain, and implacable. Great Britain's participation has given me this certitude. London has declared war on Hitler, so either he must disappear or England bite the dust."

Several days later, on September 15, concerning a project of Il Duce's to call a European conference at the end of the military operations in Poland, to establish a collective security pact among the six great European powers, he wrote: "I am sorry not to be in agreement with him this time, for in order that his project be possible, Hitler must give proof of moderation. And I do not believe him capable of that. I foresee England launching into a full-scale war against Germany, a war which will only end with one or the other being defeated. I also foresee that it will be terrible and long—very long—and that Great Britain will be victorious."

He kept to this point of view, even after long conversations with Hitler. He noted after one of these meetings on October 1 or 2, 1939: "What impressed me most is Hitler's faith in victory. His assurance tolerates no contradiction. Could he be right? It will not be so simple as he says: France and England have not yet said their last word. If war breaks out it will be a cruel war. Hitler's eyes gleam disquietingly when he discusses the means at his disposal and his methods of combat. I return from Germany convinced that the first months will allow the Germans to believe in their victory, but later on the going will get very rough indeed."

Galeazzo endeavored to consolidate friendly relations with France and England. He named an Italian Ambassador to London, Bastianini, who was later to replace him in 1943 as Secretary of

Foreign Affairs, and he maintained cordial although intransigent relations with François-Poncet, the French Ambassador to Rome. His dream was to create a bloc of neutral nations that would back up Italy and make Hitler hesitate to carry out a war elsewhere in Europe.

My husband's thinking contained one error: He believed France to be as powerful and as determined as England. However, he discovered that the French were, as even François-Poncet had said, "bizarre people who wanted to win the lottery without buying a ticket," a people whose power was only an illusion. But he only discovered this when he went to the Western Front, in France and in Belgium, on July 8 and 9, 1940, after the armistice with Italy had been requested by France and signed in Rome on June 24, 1940.

On his return from that trip Galeazzo told me that he would never have believed that the French army would fight so little. "Along the roadside," he told me, "the tanks were lined up and some of them had never fired a shot. It was a sad spectacle, and I wondered what had happened to all that power that had filled us with admiration in 1914–1918."

My father had also traveled around the Western Front. His reaction was more practical—he was bitter. He was sorry that the war had ended so quickly and that he would be obliged to sit at the negotiating table without holding some good cards, since there had been no time for the Italians to achieve any solid personal victories.

It was at that moment that my husband began to believe that victory was possible, especially after a meeting with Hitler in Munich, to which he accompanied my father, on June 18 and 19, 1940. He wrote in his notebooks: "Hitler is now a poker player who has won a big hand; and he wants to leave the table without taking any more risks. Today he spoke with such moderation and such perspicacity that we were amazed, especially after such a victory. I cannot be said to have much sympathy for him, but today I truly admired him."

176

On June 22, 1941, at three o'clock in the morning, Prince Otto von Bismarck, German Counselor of Embassy in Rome, brought my husband a long letter for my father, in which the Führer explained the reasons for his decision to attack Russia. Galeazzo informed Il Duce of its contents by telephone, for the latter was in Riccione, and my father had a violent reaction against the Germans, who continued to confront him with a completed act. Galeazzo tried in vain to contact the Soviet Embassy to notify the Ambassador of the declaration of war against them, but the latter had left for the morning to go swimming at Fregene, taking with him all the embassy personnel. It was only at about 12:30 P.M. that diplomatic relations were suspended.

My husband, my father, and I all felt that the opening of a Second Front was an error. I always remember Goering's remark: "And above all, we must not commit the fatal error of opening a Second Front against the Russians. . . ." Why did Hitler not listen to him?

From this time on, my husband became increasingly doubtful about the possibility of a victorious conclusion to the war, and, in a certain sense, a chasm began to deepen between Rome and Berlin. Mussolini and Ciano were in absolute agreement at that moment. Even their attitude toward the leaders of the Reich, whom they found offhand in their dealings with Italy, was identical.

But what could they do?

Hitler held all the cards, since he possessed all the real military power. Italy, which had launched into the North African campaign, which was working out well for the moment, desperately needed German materials. Moreover, my husband and my father had to keep a close eye on Berlin's territorial claims, notably on the Upper Adige and in Albania. Thus, they could neither provoke a crisis with Germany nor turn toward other allies. In fact, there were no other possible allies, and also neither my father nor my husband thought for one instant of not respecting the pact with Germany.

Galeazzo did try to counterbalance German designs on Albanian oil—of which he and my father had been aware since February, 1939—by persuading my father to launch military operations in Albania and in Greece. Things went well in Albania, but turned out less brilliantly in Greece, where the Germans were forced to intervene to save our troops.

Therefore, what could my father do? The only thing left for him to do would have been to withdraw from the Axis, which, as I have said, he refused to consider. He confined himself to an attempt to inspire the military with more enthusiasm, but, though the ordinary Italian soldiers fought admirably, the General Staff officers did not come up to snuff, and in 1942, our army began to give way before the enemy in Africa.

In Italy—in the face of increasingly massive bombardments every day, restrictions, blackouts, and the impression that the war would never end—morale began to sink, and, from the end of 1942, there began to be more and more talk of a conspiracy. Against whom? By whom? Obviously against the regime, but it was impossible to point the finger at anyone, for everyone seemed to be plotting something or other. There was finally so much talk about conspiracy that just a few days before his arrest my father replied to my mother, who had just been warning him about those plotting against him, "But, Rachele, don't you understand? It is not the conspirators who worry me, it's the Allied tanks."

What was my husband's attitude toward all this? I have already said that, with Germany's attack on Russia and then the entrance into the war against the Axis by the United States, Galeazzo nourished no more illusions. But he never thought of abandoning my father, that is to say, of resigning.

First of all, such an act would have served no purpose. His resignation as Foreign Minister would not have turned my father against Germany. And this, first of all, because it had been Mussolini who had wished the alliance and therefore he had to respect it. Second, because, even if my husband had been able to convince my father to abandon the Germans—which he never tried to do from the moment Italy entered the war—it would have taken less time for the German troops to occupy Italy than for the Allies to come to its defense. After all, we saw proof of this when Marshal Badoglio signed the armistice with the Allies on September 8, 1943. It took the Allies one year and a half to occupy Italy.

Thus, Ciano and Mussolini were in the same boat, and my husband never thought of abandoning it.

But how did such clearsighted men see the future and the end to all this?

There had been only one possible solution for my father, as of 1941: to sign a separate peace with Russia and, as a last resort, to negotiate with the Allies. I say as a last resort because, until 1944, after one of his last trips to Germany and after having visited the V1 and V2 bases, my father was certain that Germany could still win the war.

There was also only one political solution for my husband because he no longer had any illusions about the chances for success of the Italian army, weakened as it was by all sorts of disorders—including sabotage—or those of the German troops who, though they fought admirably, were overpowered by the Allied armies. But his solution was Italian and not international.

In my opinion, he believed that the King of Italy would finally intervene and form another government, which would give another orientation to Italy's attitude. This, I think, is what he expressed when he voted the Grandi motion during the meeting of the Inner Council on July 24, 1943.

But he never thought of getting rid of my father, and he knew that the latter was aware of his state of mind.

Also, I understand his astonishment and his chagrin on February 5, 1943, when he was summoned by Il Duce and informed that he must give up his Ministerial functions.

He wrote in his notebooks: "As soon as I entered his office, I realized that Il Duce was very embarrassed. He asked me what I wanted to do now that I was no longer Foreign Minister, and

179

then, lowering his voice, he told me that he had changed the entire government. I understand his reasons, I share them, and I cannot find the least objection to them. Among the several choices he offered me, I immediately ruled out the position as Lieutenant General in Albania, where I would be obliged to shoot those to whom I had sworn fraternity. . . . I have chosen the Ambassadorship to the Holy See. It is a restful post which can, however, offer many possibilities for the future. And the future, today more than ever before, is in God's hands.

"Abandoning the Ministry of Foreign Affairs where, during seven years—and what years!—I have given the best of myself is very difficult and I feel extremely bad about it. . . ."

But three days later, on February 8, even though for months he would from time to time rail against my father and swear furiously at him, my husband wrote about him quite differently: "Then Il Duce told me that I should consider this a rest period. 'Your turn will come again,' he added. 'Your future is in my hands and you can set your mind at ease.' "

Unfortunately, he didn't know just how apt that phrase was.

Then, my husband noted: "He asked me to visit him often, even every day. We separated on cordial terms. And I am pleased, because I like Mussolini very much indeed. And what I shall miss most will be losing touch with him."

XVII

GALEAZZO CIANO WAS NOT ELIMINATED FROM THE GOVERN-
ment because he had made critical remarks about my father or
sometimes objected in private to his decisions. After all, my
father often criticized the Führer, despite the fact that he was his
ally. The reason for Galeazzo's dismissal was that, since the
situation demanded a reorganization of the government, my
father, influenced by conspirators desiring Galeazzo's downfall,
profited from the circumstances to get rid of him.

Once Ciano had been removed from power, those who had
obtained his dismissal undertook to prove that he had been a
traitor. This was the second step in their machinations.

Clara Petacci entered into history because she was killed along
with my father, struck down at his side by a partisan. I was not

181

so much against her personally as against the scandal that she and those she protected kept alive in Italy.

I had been aware for several years of Clara's existence as my father's mistress. But I did not believe that it was serious, especially since she was not the first. My husband had been the first to speak to me about her, then several intimate friends alluded to the affair. Finally, a veritable concert of voices spread gossip about the two Petacci sisters and the sordid, dishonest financial schemes of their brother, Marcello Petacci. There was much talk too of the "most important of the Ministries," called "La Camilluccia," in reference to the house in which Clara Petacci lived, where careers were said to be made and unmade.

There was, for example, Admiral Riccardi, who did not have a good reputation in the navy—for sound reasons—and who nevertheless was appointed Undersecretary of State, solely because he was a friend of Petacci, while Felice Guarnieri, Minister of the Treasury, was dismissed because he had brought on himself the hatred of Marcello Petacci in a corrupt affair of foreign currency, gold bars, et cetera. Marcello Petacci's vulgar humor went so far beyond the usual bounds of decency that in the antechambers of the Palazzo Venezia, during Italy's reverses in the Greek campaign and in Africa, he was even heard to declare, "Everything seems to be going badly, but on the Camilluccia front everything is going very well indeed!" That gives a good idea of what the man was like.

In that sad month of November, 1942, which saw the fall of Tripoli and the rest, the scandal was such that I decided to speak up. It was not easy to do so because it is difficult as well as embarrassing to invade one's father's private life and speak to him about such intimate details.

Profiting from my husband's departure for Germany in my father's place, since the latter had to remain in Rome because of bad health, I went to lunch at the Villa Torlonia. After having succeeded in getting my mother and Irma, the classic omnipotent parlor maid, to leave my father's room, I brought up the question.

My father was in bed. I admit that I am not very diplomatic and that I do not know how to present things delicately. So I entered immediately into the heart of the matter and brusquely informed him of everything I knew: the Milan company belonging to Marcello Petacci, the fact that he was just about the only Italian to still drive around Italy in a motorcar, that he had not served one day in the army, while benefiting from surprising and flattering promotions, that it was well known that he had sold materiel to Spain. . . . I also told my father of the ridicule heaped upon him because of Clara's sister and the films she had got it into her head to make, one of which had made the Italians scream with laughter because it had been entitled *The Ways to the Heart.*

My father had been perfectly aware of all this. He told me that he had summoned Marcello Petacci and that the latter had resigned from his position as president of the company and was going to join the navy. He also declared that he was going to end his affair with Clara Petacci because no woman other than my mother had ever really meant anything to him. I could have disputed that point, but I abstained from doing so.

He thanked me for having been so frank, and I left.

In fact, I did not have much hope that I had really succeeded in my efforts. During the last years, my father and I had grown apart, and we sometimes did not see each other for months. When we did meet we always seemed to argue.

There was no repercussion from my visit during December. In January I left to go skiing, and, on February 5 (a bizarre coincidence, as it was so shortly after my conversation with him), without giving me any warning, my father dismissed my husband as Foreign Minister—obviously, the Petacci family and its accomplices had won. I had lost the first round, and my father, as usual afraid to face me in person, had profited from my absence

183

to knife in the back a man who had served him so faithfully during so many years.

It was not easy for my husband to become an Ambassador once again after having served as Foreign Minister, and everyone watched closely to see how he would take it. But we knew how to stand punishment. We began our new position with much dignity and serenity, and once again played the Ambassadorial role, the same as Galeazzo had been filling when we first met.

I remember that we had to see the diplomats whom my husband had known when he was Italy's Foreign Minister. Not only was he now merely their equal, but they had become our enemies. I had once entertained certain of the Ambassadors' wives, and it was almost comical to meet thus, in the middle of the war, on that little parcel of neutral territory that was the Vatican. Respecting the rules of decorum, but also taking into account the state of war, we simply nodded to each other.

I also recall that the private audience accorded by Pope Pius XII to Galeazzo, as a new Ambassador, as well as to myself and our children, resulted in a scene that was perhaps unique in the annals of the Holy See.

While the Pope was speaking with us my youngest son, Marzio, whom I was holding on my lap, made a sudden leap to the Pope's desk. I should have foreseen something of the kind because Marzio seemed fascinated by the gold telephone of Pius XII. The Pope leaped up at the same time as my son and attempted to protect his telephone.

For several minutes a child of six and a Pope hung onto a telephone, one trying to take it, the other trying to prevent his touching it. Pius XII shortened the audience considerably and, after several *Bene, bene, bene*'s that expressed his perplexity, he had us kneel, blessed us, and sent us away.

My husband was extremely upset. He had already been highly annoyed by the inexplicable absence of his chauffeur with the official car, which had obliged him to take the wheel of a small Fiat 500 himself. We had difficulty fitting in with Galeazzo clad in an Ambassador's dress uniform, me in a long dress, Dindina in her communion robe, et cetera. Our arrival at the Vatican must have been quite something!

But Galeazzo had not reached the end of his torment. As we left the Pope's apartments Ciccino began to reprimand his young brother for his behavior. Dindina interfered in the argument, and a dispute broke out among the three children, who raced around the heavy drapes covering the windows, while their father, to save appearances, spoke in Latin to Cardinal Maglione, the Vatican's Secretary of State, who was accompanying us.

When we had regained our jalopy, under the astonished eyes of the Swiss Guards, I heard Galeazzo swear for the first time in my presence and before the children. I must say that I understood his losing control in such circumstances.

To return to my husband's new activities, I am sure that it was difficult for him to have so little to do after so many years of hard work. I felt very sorry for him.

Then he became inured to the situation and began to interest himself in our house at Angignano, near Livorno, to which he wished to retire, since he had had enough of political life—and with reason.

During this period the Petacci scandal continued to grow. The sometimes unexpected or puzzling decisions taken by my father were attributed, rightly or wrongly, to the bad influence exercised upon him by the Petacci clique. People wondered how, at the very moment when Italy was being invaded, the country's politics could be dictated by persons like Marcello Petacci, Buffarini, et cetera.

I was not afraid of difficulties or obstacles, so I decided to attack once again. But this time I was determined not to miss my target, to be more forceful. Therefore, I asked Albini, the new Undersecretary of the Interior, to furnish me with the proofs of all Mr. Petacci's malfeasances. He gave them to me and, record in hand, I went to the Palazzo Venezia.

I showed my father the contracts that Marcello Petacci's closest friend had made with Spain, payable in gold at a higher price than the usual so that he could pocket the difference. Most of the material contracted for, moreover, had been unusable. Then I showed him the bill of sale for a villa at Merano. I informed him that in fact the order he had given Marcello Petacci to embark on a ship had been transformed into a position as director of a hospital in Venice, which was causing much gossip along the Lido.

This time my father became indignant.

"I am grateful to you for everything you have just told me," he said. "I shall never forget it. I intend to get rid of the woman immediately [she was perhaps waiting in an adjoining room during our entire conversation] and all those crooks will be arrested. What an imbecile Dr. Petacci is to have made out a bill of sale in his own name!"

He seemed more scandalized by Marcello Petacci's imbecility than by the fraudulence of his actions.

I left him, still skeptical about the results of this second visit.

I waited for two days, but nothing happened. I wrote my father a letter, then left for Florence. On my return to Rome, there was still no news about the Petaccis. I then went to Sicily to continue my service as a nurse. I sent a report from there about the disquieting state of mind of the civilian population and of the army and described as well the deplorable state of the civilian hospital, which was so bad that I even sent a special report to the Princess of Piedmont, president of the Italian Red Cross, a report that upset those concerned considerably and was not well received. The civilians were completely disoriented—they lacked electricity, means of transportation, and food and, because of the black market, prices were climbing with dizzying swiftness. They were fatalistic and resigned, two qualities that I find sadly negative when the destiny of a country is at stake.

The military was something else again. As soon as the least sound of a plane was heard the city became literally emptied out, above all of its military personnel. And at the first sound of cannon fire those who ran to save themselves first were the soldiers and the officers.

When I was sent home from Sicily, several days before the Allied landing, I finally received news of the effect of my last visit to the Palazzo Venezia.

Galeazzo recounted to me that, immediately after my visit, Clara Petacci had been sent away and all her friends and family had been panic-stricken. But two or three days later my father had allowed her to return. He had probably been convinced by some friend or collaborator who had minimized the gravity of the accusations against the Petaccis that he should do so. Now the Petacci family and their friends were filled with a violent hatred for me.

Very soon afterward the effects of this animosity began to surface: Galeazzo was accused of infidelity and treason. He went to see my father and asked to be confronted with the person who had been spreading such calumny. Papa refused, alleging that he paid no attention to such stupid and malicious gossip.

At this point we left for Livorno. In the meantime the Allies had landed in Sicily and many Italians envied the Sicilians for having reached the end of their ordeal. The situation was becoming increasingly ominous and rumors of a coup d'etat were circulating everywhere, but no one really took them seriously.

On July 15, 1943, my husband received a telephone call from Rome. He was told that my father wished to see him. Before leaving me, Galeazzo told me that there was such tension in Rome, so many contradictory rumors, that he was convinced something very grave would occur one day soon.

I recall that I answered, "If my father can remain in power only with the support of the Germans, it is better that he leave. It is no longer a question of being Fascist or anti-Fascist, but of being Italians. No matter what happens, Italy must be saved."

In saying that, I was thinking that the King could take back some of the responsibilities that he had delegated to my father and that he could help him to find a solution, since Mussolini had done so much for him.

I did not know that my ideas were going to take concrete form so quickly or in what fashion!

On July 25, at about eight o'clock in the evening, my husband telephoned me in Livorno, telling me only, "I shall send a car for you tomorrow, take the children and my mother with you. Things are stormy here."

He probably already knew that my father had been removed from power by the King after a meeting at the sovereign's private residence. My father, who had arrived in civilian clothes—as had been requested of him—innocently believed that they were going to discuss affairs of state.

He didn't even have time to open the portfolio containing his proposed list for the new government before the King, quite hysterical, shouted that he must rest and that they would talk of all that in six months. The King accompanied him to the door, shook his hand, wished him luck—and had him arrested on the spot.

I only discovered all this upon my return to Rome during the night of July 26–27, when my husband gave me all the details about what had happened since he had left Livorno on July 15. I hadn't seen him since that time. He had only telephoned to tell me that my father had not summoned him. Then he had caught the flu and had spent several days in bed. Some people have written that Galeazzo pretended to be sick in order to carry on a conspiracy. But friends, including the Marquise Delia di Bagno, went to see him and confirmed not only that he was sick but that he seemed quite calm and completely unlike someone busy plotting.

On Thursday, July 22, my husband received a summons from Carlo Scorza, the Secretary of the Fascist Party, to the Council meeting to be held on Saturday the twenty-fourth. On that Friday, at the home of Bottai, with Grandi and I don't know who else, he put the finishing touches to the text of the motion that was going to be presented, a proposal of which my father was aware insofar as its general ideas were concerned and, furthermore, had authorized its being put to a vote so as to confront each member of the Council with his responsibility.

Galeazzo ceaselessly repeated to me from the day we saw each other again, after July 24, until the end of his life, that though, in fact, Grandi could be distrusted, almost no one else among those who voted for the proposal had any intention of betraying Il Duce. For the most part, they were acting, as was he, in good faith. And my father reaffirmed this declaration when I saw him again—no one had been in league with those who staged the coup d'etat.

I remained tranquilly with my children during the meeting of the Inner Council and my father's session with the King, followed by his arrest on the sovereign's orders. During the night of July 24–25, Livorno had suffered a violent bombardment, and we had found ourselves in a shelter with, among others, the terrified family of a police officer who had found nothing better to calm them down than to say, "Don't be afraid. Everything will be all right, since the countess is with us." As though my presence could blind the English pilots who, contrary to the American pilots, who killed you within several minutes during one single bombardment, gave you all the time in the world to die by flying and then reflying over the city to take better aim at their objectives in the flashes of light caused by their bombs.

At around five o'clock on the morning of Sunday, the twenty-fifth, my father tried to reach me by telephone. But he did not succeed, and I was only informed of his call later during the day by the colonel of the constabulary, Factuel. I don't know if the arrest mechanism had already been put in motion or whether the telephone really didn't function.

I slept badly on the night of July 25–26. I knew nothing of the dramas unfolding, but I had a nasty boil and was very feverish. Galeazzo's aunt telephoned me to say, "I'm afraid because there

189

are some men outside shouting that they are going to break everything." I rushed to her house but I saw no one around except for several passersby, who looked at me strangely. They knew what had happened, and they must have thought that I was truly a thoughtless female. On the morning of the twenty-sixth my car did not arrive, and telephone communications were cut. During the morning a captain of the constabulary came to our villa to tell me that we must leave by train. I was more and more intrigued and puzzled.

At about two in the afternoon I succeeded in getting a newspaper and learned for the first time that my father was no longer in power—a fact known to everyone in Italy save myself.

"What are we going to do?" asked one of my sons. "Are we going to be killed like the Tsar and his children?"

"The least that can happen is that your father will lose his job," I replied, "or we will be exiled if not sent to prison. The worst that can happen is that we will be killed. But whatever happens, we must prepare ourselves for a new way of life."

I who had found life as the wife of a diplomat and Minister far too monotonous was going to be well served!

The return to Rome by train was long and painful. My boil was hurting terribly, and my mother-in-law, unaware of the gravity of the situation, had dressed up as though she were going to a garden party. On the supply-train wagons we passed I saw written "Down with Il Duce!" "Down with Mussolini!" "Long live the King!" "Long live Badoglio!" Ciccino and Dindina had tears in their eyes, because they could read the statements. Marzio, the youngest, was not old enough to understand anything, and he behaved like a cooped-up puppy. Childhood and old age can be very much alike.

The train entered the station in Rome four hours late, at around midnight. Irony of ironies, our carriage stopped in front of the red carpet used for dignitaries!

We were escorted by constabulary officers. One of them, once we were in the car, reproached me for not having told Il Duce of the people's sentiments and the truth about the situation. I couldn't reveal that my father had not listened to me for years and that it would have been like preaching in the desert. I asked them where my father was and they answered, "At Rocca delle Caminate."

The city was decked out as it had been for the taking of Addis Ababa. We were treated with great courtesy and taken to the house.

When my husband saw us he embraced us so fervently that I wondered why he was being so emotional. Later he told me that he had seen the outburst of the crowd the day before, in the Piazza Venezia, and he had been afraid that something might happen to us during the trip.

Once my mother-in-law and the children had been sent to bed, we sat alone and talked. He told me that he would never have suspected that the fall of Il Duce and of his regime would be so complete, or that it would be greeted with such frenzy. People embraced in the streets, the party insignia were knocked down and slashed to pieces as were the photos of my father. "We haven't the least chance of survival if we remain in Italy," he concluded.

The next day he met with General Ambrosio and discussed his resignation as Ambassador to the Holy See. He also requested passports for us so that we might go abroad. That same evening the Minister of Justice, Acquarone, came to the house and told Galeazzo that by order of His Majesty he was to remain as Ambassador to the Vatican. Although very skeptical, Galeazzo obeyed instructions.

I remember that during their conversation they discussed the possible consequences of recent events. When they expressed their misgivings regarding the reaction of the Germans to the news of my father's elimination I said to them, "If the Germans react, I will serve as a buffer. But if the Allies are the ones to arrive, perhaps then *you* can do something for me."

In fact, none of us realized yet how grave the situation was.

Two days after Acquarone's visit the King had my husband

informed that it might be better if he were to resign. On the following Saturday, July 31, Galeazzo handed over his responsibilities to his successor, whose name I have forgotten.

In the interval, except for the fact that we could not leave Rome, we were subjected to no restrictions. All of our friends came to see us, some out of curiosity, others to thumb their noses at the police guarding us, the majority because they truly loved us.

Outdoors the air was heavy and suffocating. My husband did not leave the house for two weeks. The press had begun its classic campaign of calumnies, mostly against us, and in the streets the people continued to destroy, break, trample everything in sight, including the statues of my father-in-law, Costanzo Ciano. They also began to talk of our enormous, illicit fortune—the famed billion. Not a day, an hour, a minute passed without a new affront being inflicted upon us. I even learned later that one of our friends, who had gone to her hairdresser at Riccione, barely escaped from the place when her coiffeur wanted to shave her head. The Italians behaved neither with responsibility, nor moderation, nor dignity.

However, the population became increasingly curious as the days passed. They could not understand why Mussolini had been eliminated by the King and replaced by Badoglio simply in order to continue fighting alongside the Germans. And Badoglio's new proclamation as head of the Italian government was like a cold slap in the face as well as a stimulant to resist the new regime and the King.

Then the men in power gave the people something to play with—the Fascists against whom they took up the chase. One evening the Minister of Foreign Affairs, Guariglia, remarked to Princess Colonna, "Since we cannot give the Italians peace, we must give them something to amuse them and help them to forget what is going on. So we are giving them Fascists to devour."

Everyone advised us to flee. But how? Guariglia became very difficult, and the passports we had requested never arrived.

My husband began to despair and there were days when he spoke of suicide. He could not support the idea that he had contributed to my father's arrest, even if he had voted in good faith. My battle was difficult!

I occasionally received news of my family. I learned that Vittorio had succeeded in fleeing to Germany. Houses were starting to be searched. I was not so much afraid for us as for our children. What would happen to them if we disappeared?

If the men in power had been anti-Fascists it would have been easier to bear. But it was disgusting to see Johnny-come-latelies, who had eaten at our dinner table for twenty years, who had reaped all the advantages possible from Fascism, who had shared responsibility with us, turn against us now like serpents.

On August 21, after having discussed our problems at length, we decided to ask the Germans for help. They were the only ones who could get us out of Italy. We were furious with the King, and with Badoglio and his gang.

I thought of writing a letter to Hitler, but we preferred finally to contact one of the German officials in Rome. I knew Lt. Col. Eugen Dollmann, the head of the S.S. in Rome. He could perhaps be of great assistance to us, but we first had to reach him.

I asked one of our best friends, Candido Bigliardi, an Admiral, who held an important post in the Italian navy and had the possibility of reaching Dollmann without too much trouble, to help us.

Up until the end of 1973 Admiral Bigliardi was president of an extremely important company making armaments for the navy. Clear-thinking, with a good head on his shoulders, Candido Bigliardi was one of Galeazzo Ciano's friends when he was Secretary at the Consulate in Shanghai, during his first sojourn in China. Bigliardi was in command of one of the Italian warships which cruised up and down the Yangtze to serve as protection for the Italian colony living in China. After his return to Italy he occupied several important posts and even had his ship sunk under him in combat. Then he directed the Operations section of the navy and was responsible for the celebrated missions of the Italian "frog-torpedo" men who caused great damage to Allied ships with their explosives.

After September 8 he himself put an end to his official functions by accompanying the King of Italy to his point of embarkation, then resigning from the navy. He reentered the service only after the end of the war.

Admiral Bigliardi recounts, "In fact, from 1940 on I saw very little of Galeazzo Ciano. He had important responsibilities that kept him busy and I had my missions, which kept me away from Rome for long periods of time. However, each time that I did happen to be in the capital, Galeazzo freed himself for a time so that we could talk together.

"I did not know much about the subtleties of politics, but when I saw Galeazzo in those last days, I realized that the atmosphere in Rome had become extremely menacing. Our last conversation before the coup d'etat took place several days before the meeting of the Inner Council. Filippo Anfuso met with us. He had been Galeazzo's principal private secretary at the Foreign Ministry and was now Minister at the Italian Embassy in Budapest. I remember him saying, 'You are all crazy. Do you really believe that if a motion hostile to Il Duce's policies was voted at the Inner Council it would not have grave consequences? Everyone will be swept out if that occurs—Il Duce, the government, the regime, you! And don't think it would be possible to govern Italy while maintaining Fascism without Mussolini. That is impossible! Without him, you will all be ruined!'

"Galeazzo disagreed. He believed that if the Grandi motion were voted, Il Duce could share the governing of the country with the King. This was the first time that I had heard anyone speak of the crisis in such precise terms. Until now there had been only vague rumors floating about.

"When I learned that Il Duce had been arrested, I dashed over to the Cianos'. Galeazzo was terribly upset. What Filippo Anfuso had predicted seemed to have come about.

"The first few days he kept relatively calm, but as time passed he became increasingly nervous.

"Edda Ciano accompanied me one evening as far as the elevator, and asked me to help her to see Dollmann.

"I replied that she was mad, since the Germans could not bear her husband!

"She replied, 'I know that, but they are the only ones who can give us a plane to fly to Spain. You cannot imagine what I must go through to keep up Galeazzo's spirits. It is becoming impossible! I would rather run the risk of facing the Germans, and perhaps my name will help a bit . . .'

"Edda gave me a letter in which she asked Dollmann to have confidence in me and to listen to the message I was bringing him, and I met with the chief of the S.S. in Rome. Our encounter took place in a hotel in the center of the city where he lived with the proprietress of the establishment. Dollmann listened, then told me that he would look into the question.

"Several days later he informed me that he would receive Countess Ciano on such and such an evening and that I must accompany her to an apartment away from the center of the capital.

"On the appointed evening, when the car stopped at the Via Angelo Secchi [where the Cianos' apartment was located], the sirens began to sound the alert. We leaped into the car and went to meet Dollmann. Later I learned that it was the Germans who had sounded the alert to hide our departure and arrival. My mission was over. Countess Ciano had made contact with Dollmann.

"Now the second stage in Countess Ciano's plan began—to succeed in leaving Italy with her husband and children."

Dollmann informed me that, Berlin having given its approval, it was Commander Kappler of the S.S. who was now in charge of organizing our departure.

A week after my first meeting with Dollmann a German officer dressed in civilian clothes came to the house, bearing a bouquet of flowers, to tell me when and how we would leave by plane. On August 27, a Friday, I was to leave the house with the children as though we were taking a walk; a car would pick us up after several minutes. My husband was to leave several moments later, and another car would stop for him.

On the morning of August 27, carrying my purse, which held only a few jewels, we left the house, looking very casual. The children wore the same clothes they had on when they had been playing in Livorno. Dindina carried a celluloid duck. So we really looked as though we were simply taking a stroll.

Our house had been closely watched for days. Raimondo Lanza, one of our closest friends, had been astonished that we were still in Rome when he had seen us the previous day. "In a day or two Galeazzo will be arrested and taken to the island of Ponza," he said to me.

Perhaps the Italians would have liked to use Galeazzo to enter into contact with the Allies. Caught short by their coup d'etat, Badoglio's people did not know to whom to address themselves in order to negotiate an armistice. They sent people in all directions, which served only to negate what they were trying to do and showed the Allies to what point we were in a state of confusion. If Galeazzo had been utilized as an intermediary, he would perhaps still be alive.

When I reached the street the guards placed around our house had disappeared.

The car met us at the Piazza Santiago del Chile. We picked up my husband at the German Academy. He too had left the house without any problem.

From there we were transferred to a military truck and driven to the Ciampino airfield. The truck backed up to the door of the plane, whose motors were already turning. We took off, and the first thing we did was to pin our Fascist insignia onto our lapels once again. I had told the children of our trip only one half-hour before our departure from the house; they behaved magnificently.

The flight was normal except for the cold and the dirt. When we asked where we were going we were told that we were landing

196

at Munich for lunch and would fly on to Spain from there, with a probable stop in Berlin to pick up false passports made out in names other than our own.

General Hellstein, commander of the S.S. in Bavaria, was awaiting us at the airport in Munich. We were conducted by car to Allmannshausen, several hundred meters from Starnberg Lake, where a villa was put at our disposal.

I was surprised at this because we had been told that we would be leaving immediately for Spain. I was even more surprised when General Hellstein informed us that we would be receiving ration cards for food and clothing.

"My God!" said Galeazzo, turning to me. "I think they are counting on keeping us here for some time."

I tried to argue about these arrangements, claiming that they were unnecessary because of the promises that had been made to me in Rome.

Two days later Himmler's right-hand man, Kaltenbrunner, in a note delivered along with some flowers from Ribbentrop, asked to be received. When he arrived he told me that the Führer wished to see me. I was astonished because he spoke only to me and seemed to ignore my husband's existence. I felt sorry for Galeazzo and began to feel a violent antipathy for Kaltenbrunner. I was not used to being considered the head of the family—I had always been number two.

It was decided that on the following Tuesday, August 31, I would go to Hitler's general headquarters, flying in a private plane. In the meantime, Major Bohle of the S.S. and Marshal Leckner, who lived in our villa, declared unceasingly that within two days we would be happy and safe in Spain.

On Monday, August 30, we had our photographs taken for the false passports, for which my husband wore a fake moustache. He was to be an Argentinian of Italian origin and I Margaret Smith, an Englishwoman born in Shanghai. Even the children had their false papers. All this was merely a tragicomedy, since as regards passports all we ever received were the photos.

On Tuesday, August 31, I flew off to see Hitler, accompanied by a functionary from the Ministry of Foreign Affairs. The flight was a nightmare of bad storms, so I drank some cognac and took pills against airsickness, which only succeeded in making me dizzy. My flight companion could think of nothing better to bolster my morale than to explain that what we were forced to go through now was nothing compared to what the Reich would have to endure from the Russians at the end of the war!

We landed five hours later. Dr. Schmidt and several other persons were waiting to take me by car to general headquarters. We made a stop at the Führer's train so that I might wash and generally freshen up. There I ran into Dornsberg, a very curious German diplomat.

After about half an hour I reached the Führer's residence, a group of barracks scattered through the forest.

I have already recounted what occurred at our meeting, but I did not mention one point. Once we had discussed the Inner Council and my father's arrest, I told Hitler what I thought of our being held in Germany and added that we were adamant, no matter what the cost, about reaching Spain.

The Führer answered with a tirade in German. "The Führer has no intention of keeping you here against your will. However, he hopes that you are aware of the dangers facing you, particularly in Spain. That country is not serious and certainly not loyal. You might be kidnapped by the English."

I replied that I didn't care a fig for what might happen to us just so long as we were able to enjoy a little freedom, that we had only one desire—to be lost in the crowd, anonymous and apolitical.

At that point I asked him if the money we had brought with us could be changed into pesetas. He told me to give it to his secretary, who would do the necessary.

I left Hitler after a conversation lasting over an hour. Having seen his gifts for my father, I was convinced that the Führer had been informed about everything that had occurred in Italy and that he was determined not only to free my father, but also to avenge him.

I spent the night in the Führer's train, where I saw Vittorio, who had come from Königsberg but had not been told by the Germans—because of their habitual love for secrecy—whom he was going to meet. I was so certain that we were to leave for Spain shortly that I told my brother he could count on me if he needed anything.

The next day the Führer came to wish me a happy birthday. We spoke again of Spain and he promised that he would send a plane in five days to take my husband to meet him. I returned to Allmannshausen confident and reassured.

Alas, the sole plane to come was that sent on October 19 to fly Galeazzo directly to Verona.

Two days later I sent the Führer a letter thanking him for his friendly reception and reminding him that I needed help for our flight to Spain. I also asked for news of my father. My letter was never answered. I sent another to Himmler, insisting on Spain, and a third to Ribbentrop thanking him for his flowers. I could not ask Ribbentrop for help since he had let me know in no uncertain terms what he thought of Galeazzo.

The waiting began—for Galeazzo's plane, for arrangements regarding our departure for Spain, for those famous passports.

Whenever we asked questions, the reply was the same— that we were the Führer's guests and had nothing to worry about.

Life at Allmannshausen became increasingly difficult: bad food, disagreeable personnel, only relative liberty since the S.S. were always with us.

Galeazzo's nerves began to crack from September fifth on, and mine faltered soon afterward. But I still could not believe that the Germans had tricked us.

Major Bohle, a specialist in mysterious operations, left and returned to Italy. His place was taken by a young S.S. from Berlin, Major Scheiber, who had a handsome car and was full of amiable attention to me such as finding American cigarettes, gin, playing cards, and pajamas. He liked the good things in life and was quite charming.

As to Spain, there was no further mention of it.

My children's nurse also left, alleging that the house was too disorganized for her. The food degenerated completely, not because there wasn't enough of it, but because the best of it remained in the kitchen where the Lisas, Hanses, and others held open house for their friends.

Major Scheiber then left and was replaced by another S.S., Major Otto.

I had never really hated anyone until I met Otto. A defrocked priest, depraved and heartless, he immediately gave us the impression that we were prisoners. He came to an agreement with the servants that our life should be rendered more difficult. He did not permit my husband to go to Munich and he limited my movements; Marzio had a little cat that he tried to hide so that it would not be brutally kicked, but Otto took it and killed it; even when they went to bed, the children were escorted to their room by an S.S.

We began to think of suicide once we realized that we were in fact prisoners.

The armistice that Badoglio had signed with the Allies on September 8 was the reason for this change in attitude. Now we were regarded as traitors.

On the night of September 12 we were listening to the radio when the telephone rang. Lisa took the call, and several moments later, she returned, radiant with emotion, shouting, "Il Duce is free!"

Galeazzo and I were overcome with delight. I was so happy that, obeying some need or other to thank God for such marvelous news, I took a brooch that I was wearing and gave it to our maid. I believed that our nightmare was over.

The next morning I had only one idea in mind—to see my father, embrace him, bring him the moral support that he certainly needed after the trials he had suffered.

But that was easier said than done. I stormed about, demanding a means of transportation to go to him, but ran up against a sort of impassable wall, a barrier of inertia, smiles, promises to do the necessary never put into practice.

Finally, beside myself, I decided to take the bull by the horns and oblige the German authorities to do something positive. I ran out onto the road leading from Allmannshausen to Munich, and, installing myself on a bench, I declared to the S.S. who were constantly following me, "You can tell your superiors that I will not budge from here until the car that I have requested to take me to Il Duce has arrived!"

Once again my stubbornness succeeded. As though a magic wand had been waved, an automobile stopped before me only a few minutes after the S.S. had left to inform their superiors of my decision.

On the Führer's orders, the Printz Karl Palatz, an old but comfortable residence, had been placed at my father's disposal in Munich so that he might rest for a few days and await my mother, who had been placed under "house arrest" at Rocca delle Caminate the day after my father's arrest and was now being escorted by an S.S. unit to a plane that would fly her to Munich.

When I arrived at Printz Karl Palatz I realized that my visit had already been announced. Kaltenbrunner and Otto Skorzeny were in my father's antechamber to keep away any visitors who might be in the way. It would be exaggerating to say that my arrival gave them pleasure, but they were perfectly courteous and, after several minutes' wait because my father was in conference, they ushered me into his office.

We were both sincerely moved, and his haggard face showed to what point he had suffered morally during his forty-five days of detention. His eyes were sad, filled with incredulity as a result of the volte-face of the Badoglio government. We would have liked to speak longer, but now that the news of his liberation had spread, there were many requests to see him, emanating from the Italian colony living in Germany. Also, my father intended to

201

address the population by radio as soon as possible to try to put an end to the absurd situation created by Badoglio, which was about to cut Italy in two and impel the Germans to make the Italians suffer the consequences of his government's attitude. After all, Badoglio's actions had made Italy betray everyone—the partisans of peace as well as the leaders of the Reich. Later, moreover, I was given proof that my father had succeeded in saving Italy in the nick of time from destruction by Germany when he accepted power once again.

I left again for Allmannshausen but the next morning returned to the Printz Karl Palatz. And this time I had no difficulty in obtaining a car. We spoke of my father's detention, his liberation, and, of course, of Galeazzo.

I repeated to him everything that my husband had told me under oath, and I asked him to see Galeazzo and have a frank talk with him.

Papa accepted the idea, and then he said what I have declared earlier, "Most of those who voted the Grandi motion did so in good faith, though they were idiots. The only real traitors are Grandi, Bottai, Federzoni, Albini, and Bastianini."

Galeazzo saw my father several days later. The greeting was warm and they embraced with emotion. Then they were closeted together for some time. Upon leaving my father's office Galeazzo seemed quite serene. He told me that he had explained his role to my father, who had seemed to believe him, and that he had asked to be permitted to return to Italy and work in no matter what capacity, including going into the air force. According to my husband, Papa had agreed to this.

The lunch that we all had together was not overfriendly, and the looks my mother gave Galeazzo did nothing to relax the tension. But I had the impression that my father and I had found each other again and that, despite the errors committed, we could now perhaps battle side by side as in the old days.

As a little sidelight on history, I shall recount how I saw my father try to constitute his government, during one of my visits to Karl Palatz. My father had just called Bern to speak to Massimo Magistrati, my brother-in-law—that is to say, the husband of Galeazzo's sister now dead—and ask if he would agree to accept a position in his government. Magistrati, who was Ambassador to Bern, was prudent and shrewd. At first he pretended not to recognize Il Duce, and then, when it became evident that it was my father's voice at the other end of the wire, he pretended that he could neither hear nor understand what was being said to him. Finally my father hung up—he had understood. However, Anfuso as well as Galeazzo Pini, my husband's cousin, replied immediately in the affirmative.

Despite my father's return to power, life at Allmannshausen did not become easier. The personnel changed constantly, but as though in line with a predetermined plan. After the apparently disgusted nurse and the amiabilities of Scheiber, we had suffered the brutal behavior of an Otto. Now we endured the impersonal correctness of a hostess—Frau Beetz, who stayed on with us till the end.

About September 20 Galeazzo began to talk to me of his notebooks and other documents that he had hidden in a safe place in Italy. Since he was so uncertain about how things were going to turn out, he began to have only one idea in his head—to recover them so that he could, if need be, communicate their contents to the world at large and so make known his true role. But, in order to recover those documents, it was necessary to go to Italy, and I was the only person to be able to do that.

Thus I decided to leave for Italy, but I soon realized that there was a great difference between planning such a trip and making it—for I needed the authorization of the Germans once again. And they did not seem at all disposed to give it to me.

I seemed to be hitting my head against a stone wall once more. Finally, in distress, I demanded of my father that he intervene with the authorities. It has been said that I made this request during a stormy meeting with him. That is untrue. I merely telephoned to him—though I admit that the conversation was vehement.

"If you can't get me the authorization to go to Italy, what on earth can you do? I tell you that I want to leave and I will leave!" I shouted.

My father, like the Germans, gave in for the sake of peace and quiet, and he promised that I would obtain without delay the documents and visas necessary for leaving Germany. Several days later, not without new recriminations on my part against the chief of the S.S. at Allmannshausen, I received the *Ausweis* that would permit me to pass the frontier.

That document, which I have saved, was made out in the name of Emilia Santos. Officially I was a nurse going on a mission to Rome in the company of two other nurses. Doubtless they deemed that two companions were not enough because the Gestapo added a "guardian angel" in the form of a priest who had been ordered to dog my footsteps faithfully. Each time he left the compartment he locked me in, and each time I went to the bathroom he accompanied me and waited outside the door.

The journey from Munich to Rome was not at all restful. First of all, the train that I took on September 27, 1943, was a military convoy en route to Cassino; then, like all military trains at that time, we had many stops, aerial attacks, et cetera, which made us lose hours.

I finally arrived in Rome, exhausted and filthy but rather happy. I was finally in my own country again and now hoped to find faithful friends, talk with them, and put my plans into action.

During all the time that I had spent in Allmannshausen the only person I had been permitted to see was Myriam Blanc, the most faithful of friends, who had been allowed in by the Gestapo possibly because she was teaching in Germany of her own free will, and so they trusted her. Myriam Blanc, with whom I had spent the day preceding my departure from Munich, was indefatigably devoted.

Once I arrived in Rome, despite the presence of the two nurses, who were also staying at the Hotel Atlantico on the Via Cavour, my first project was to renew contact with friends who could help me. I telephoned first to Lola Giovanelli and to Delia di Bagno, telling them both that I hoped to see them.

The first replied in a manner that took me two months back in time, when our relations had become less intimate because Galeazzo had been compromised and was no longer useful.

"You know, Edda," she said to me, sounding embarrassed, "I would prefer that you not come to the house. We have placed a sign on our door marked 'Embassy of Argentina.' So, you see, it could be awkward if you were seen here."

I understood and did not insist. The second, on the other hand—Delia—warmed the cockles of my heart.

"Edda," she exclaimed when she recognized my voice, "where are you? Don't move, I'll come to get you and take you to the house! You can rest with me and then we shall see about your needs."

Several minutes later I found her waiting for me on the Via Cavour, and, for the first time in two months, I felt myself surrounded by friendship, affection, and sincerity. And how good that feeling was!

After I had explained what I planned to do, neither Delia, her husband, nor her mother, the Duchess of Laurenzana, hesitated in the slightest about helping me. The duchess was too old to launch into this adventure with me, but her encouragement and the warm tone of her voice touched me profoundly. From first to last, Delia was my accomplice, to such an extent that she suffered a backlash from the Germans when I succeeded in reaching Switzerland. When interrogated personally by General Wolff, commander of the S.S. in Northern Italy, she never weakened or betrayed me.

My first objective was to find Galeazzo's notebooks, which he had told me were in the safekeeping of his uncle Gino, who was living at Ponte a Moriano near Lucca, where my mother-in-law had a house. It was complicated for me to reach the village, even though on the face of it there was nothing to prevent me from going there. On the one hand, I preferred to keep out of the way of the Germans, who would have considerably hindered my search; on the other hand, it was not easy to find means of transportation since individuals needed a special authorization to drive a car.

Delia and I were innocent enough to think that since my father had been freed and had returned to power we could ask the Minister of the Interior for help. I must have been truly naïve to have imagined for one instant that Buffarini-Guidi, who had installed himself at the Viminal as soon as the Germans had once again taken control of Rome, could help me!

When he received me in his office, where I also saw Pavolini, not only did he tell me that he could not furnish me with a car, but he declared that it would be better for me if I did not "make waves."

Nevertheless, I had to leave for Ponte a Moriano as quickly as possible, for I could neither go to a hotel since my papers were not in order, nor move into my own apartment because it had been sealed (which did not prevent it from being burgled). It was a paradoxical situation: I was Mussolini's daughter, I had barely escaped being arrested by my father's enemies when he had been dismissed from power, and now that he had returned, those very same men who were supposed to obey him were putting spokes in my wheels. It is true, of course, that being Galeazzo Ciano's wife rendered me suspect to the Fascists, while if I had been merely Il Duce's daughter, all doors would have been open to me. In any case, I was determined to have my way despite the Pavolinis and the Buffarini-Guidis.

I stayed on with Delia di Bagno and finally found a car to drive to Ponte a Moriano.

Once I arrived there—catastrophe! After the usual sentimental greetings my mother-in-law informed me that the documents Galeazzo had entrusted to Zio Gino had disappeared. The latter had buried them at the foot of a tree in his garden, and someone seeing him do so and certainly believing them to be cash or jewels had dug them up and stolen them.

I was prostrate with grief. My husband had put all his hopes on those papers so as to justify himself in the eyes of history, and now they no longer existed.

For the first time in months Providence intervened—after several days the documents magically reappeared. In reality, this must be attributed to my mother-in-law, who told everyone in the village that a package containing family papers had been lost and that she was ready to pay a handsome sum to whoever returned it. Several days later she found the package lying at the foot of the garden gate. It was a miracle that the person who had taken the papers had not destroyed them upon finding that there was no money. As Galeazzo said, the ways of the Lord are mysterious!

Once in possession of the notebooks, which covered the period during which my husband had been Minister of Foreign Affairs, I still had to find the notes concerning all the Ciano-Ribbentrop conversations and a file called "Germany," which treated the relations between Italy and Germany and to which were attached some personal documents.

According to my mother-in-law, they were in Rome, where Zio Gino had hidden them. So I left for the capital. Zio Gino gave me everything in due course.

Luck was with me now, and though my apartment had been burgled, everything had not been stolen. Also, the jewels I had entrusted to some friends were at my disposal. Then, thanks to one of those persons that destiny places in one's path when it wishes to help, I ran into Candido Bigliardi, the man who had established our contact with Dollmann when we wished to flee to Spain.

I asked him for assistance, and he gave it without the least hesitation. He had our apartment broken into by some sailors so that I was able to recover many objects, which I then moved to a safer place.

As I mentioned earlier, some of my friends had refused to receive me. But all those to whom I had entrusted my jewels were absolutely honest, although they could very well have kept all or a part of what I had given them, as did some of my mother's friends. Nevertheless, though they gave me back my possessions, they refused to receive me. Try to understand people!

My mission relating to the documents was terminated. But Galeazzo and my children were still in Germany.

I left Rome for Rocca delle Caminate, where my father had been staying since the first days in October. Upon my arrival I met with Marshal Graziani, Buffarini-Guidi and several Ministers belonging to the new government constituted by my father. My conversation with those men made a curious impression on me. When I spoke of my father, of my mother, of subjects other than my husband, they were amiable and answered pleasantly, considering me as Il Duce's daughter. But as soon as Galeazzo Ciano was mentioned I became the wife of a "traitor," and they became distant, cutting short any possibility of conversation.

At Rocca delle Caminate I learned nothing new from my father except that my children were with my mother and that nothing had been decided about Galeazzo. My father advised me to get some rest and promised that he would take care of all our problems once the new government began to function effectively.

Thus, I left again for Rome and, once there, I agreed to follow the advice of Dr. Frugoni, who recommended that I install myself at Ramiola to regain my strength.

That occurred on or about October 15. Four days later, on October 19, the news reached me that my husband had returned to Italy and that immediately upon his arrival in Verona he had been imprisoned.

XVIII

Galeazzo Ciano's arrest was, in fact, merely the confirmation of a state of affairs that had existed since his arrival in Germany. And, contrary to the situation in August, when he had been flown to Munich with his family rather than to Spain, on October 19, 1943, Ciano knew what was awaiting him when the plane flying him back from Germany landed in Italy.

He had, moreover, said to Major Hottl, who had come to inform him of what would occur upon his return to Italy, "What does that matter, since I will be back in my own country!"

Did Il Duce's former Foreign Minister think that his father-in-law, who had acceded to Galeazzo's desire to return to Italy, could save him from the worst? Had he received assurances of this from Mussolini? No one knows, and it is hardly probable that we shall ever find out anything further. But one thing is certain: Galeazzo Ciano had only one idea in mind—to leave the Reich as soon as possible and no matter what the cost, even though it meant being incarcerated in an Italian prison cell.

It is obvious that the plane that took off from Munich in the early afternoon of October 19, 1943, carried on board a passenger who was already aware of one part of what lay before him. Life is so very strange! That man who had fought with all his might to escape arrest in his own country had finally decided, with relief one might say, to submit to that fate in order to escape from the clutches of an ally whom he had never liked! Some might call it a miscalculation based on no rhyme or reason, when in fact the coherence of Ciano's thought and acts was exemplary.

Accompanying Galeazzo Ciano, who was dressed in a light gray flannel suit and a tan raincoat, were ten S.S. men in battle dress, with machine guns cradled in their arms, and a pretty, blond woman of some thirty-odd years, with light gray eyes and rosy fingernails.

Seated next to Il Duce's son-in-law, that young woman, who entered history under the name of Frau Beetz or Felicitas Beetz, was called at the time Hilde Felicitas Burkhardt. She was the wife of a Luftwaffe colonel and also a special agent in the service of Heinrich Himmler, chief of the S.S. and of the Gestapo. Her job was to accompany Ciano and get out of him the maximum number of secrets.

Shaken by air pockets, the plane descended over Verona, which was blurred by rain and lost in the evening dusk.

His forehead glued to the porthole, replying only in monosyllables to the remarks of his companion, Mussolini's former Foreign Minister was lost in thought as he imagined the pilot's maneuvers at the controls as he threaded in and out between the mass of mountain peaks.

When they landed, the plane came to a stop not far from a dark blue car from which men, wearing uniforms unknown to Ciano, descended. They were members of the Italian Social Republic's militia.

"Galeazzo Ciano, you are under arrest," declared one of them who had taken several steps in his direction.

"I am aware of that," replied Ciano laconically.

Less than one hundred kilometers away, at Gargnano, a small town on the banks of Lake Garda, where the government of the Social Republic was installed, Edda Ciano, who had been informed of her husband's arrival and arrest in Verona, asked her father to receive her.

XIX

IT WAS NOT EASY TO REACH MY FATHER. EVERYONE, INCLUDING my family, had put obstacles in the way, for they knew why I had come. But once again, in spite of the Fascists and the S.S., I succeeded in talking with him alone just two days after my husband's arrival in Verona.

"It is true," said my father. "Galeazzo has been arrested and is imprisoned in Verona. Actually, he may be safer there than elsewhere. There will undoubtedly be a trial, but don't worry, I shall make the necessary provisions for the outcome."

I then asked if I might see Galeazzo, and my father, having no reason to refuse me such an authorization, granted my request. However, once more I was on my own and obliged to manage things by myself. No one in my family or among my father's collaborators offered to accompany me to Verona. The sole person to reveal any courage was Eraldo Monzeglio, a famous football player of the time, a friend of my brother's who had faithfully followed my father to the North. After my interview with my father at Gargnano, Eraldo and I left for Verona.

At the Prefecture in Verona, Prefect Cosmin received me not only coldly but with great hostility. However, he had to obey the order written and signed by my father that I placed before him.

I had a new encounter with Buffarini-Guidi, who, I don't know why, felt it necessary to tell me that he would visit my husband in two or three days and that I need not worry. His visit never took place, and in any case I don't know what good it would have done Galeazzo.

I went to the Scalzi prison in the company of Cosmin and was received by the director, who preceded me into the buildings. I can still hear the keys turning in the locks and see myself mounting the staircase to reach the second floor, where my husband was imprisoned in Cell Number 27. Anyone who has made that sort of visit would understand what I felt at that moment.

It was the first time that I had seen Galeazzo since our separation at Allmannshausen. I had many, many things to tell him, but it is astonishing how, in such dramatic circumstances and in the presence of others accompanying you, one becomes stupid and mute.

I could think of nothing else to say to him than, "How are you? Do you need anything?"—banalities of the worst kind, when we had so much to discuss, such as his papers, the children, his situation.

Despite the presence of the director and the prefect, I did succeed in murmuring to him, as I kissed him good-bye, that I had his papers in my possession and that they were safe. Along with my visit and my promise to return, it was certainly the information that gave him the most pleasure.

My promise to come back turned out to be much more difficult to fulfill than I knew at the time. Galeazzo's imprisonment had altered everything. Yes, he was back in his own country, but he was a prisoner, and thus it was up to me to take action. During my conversations in Rome with Buffarini-Guidi in Rocca delle Caminate and with certain Ministers in my father's new government, I had had proof of the fact that my husband was not at all persona grata. Therefore, I had to act rapidly to try to get him freed.

I was also concerned with my children's safety from reprisals, which meant that I had to find a way to get them to Switzerland. This was made all the more complicated by the fact that they were living with my mother, who was residing in a château on the outskirts of Munich put at her disposal by the Führer until her return to Italy.

I could not run the risk of returning to Germany because I was no longer under the moral protection of my father there. Also, I did not want to leave Italy because of Galeazzo's situation, since I had no illusions about how most of the Italian government's leaders felt about him. Finally, my mother continued to declare that Galeazzo ought to be judged and punished, and she even said this in the presence of my children, so that I was convinced she would not permit me to take them away from her.

Thus, I was obliged to plot carefully and to have someone willing to assist me in reaching my end. That someone was my brother Vittorio. Since he sometimes served as liaison between my father and the Führer's headquarters, I thought of asking him to profit from one of these trips to bring the children back to Italy.

In November of 1943 I asked him to render me that service, explaining that I could not tolerate their absence. Vittorio was not at all happy with this mission, but he did not refuse my request and furthermore did not try to convince me to change my mind or require any pressure on my part to assure his acquiescence.

Vittorio's first attempt failed. In Berlin he asked for and obtained a meeting with the Undersecretary of State for Foreign Affairs. During the first part of the conversation, which began in the hotel where he was residing and continued in the air-raid shelter of the establishment because of a bombardment, they spoke of diverse things. Then, at a certain moment, Vittorio brought up, in a quite roundabout way, the question of the children.

Immediately a wall sprang up between Vittorio and his companion. The latter became evasive, talked about the tranquillity of the region in which my mother was residing, described the terrible bombardments throughout other areas of Germany and Italy, but that was all. Vittorio did not insist.

He was not proud when he returned to see me.

"Well, what happened?" I asked him. "Is this the way you keep your promises? Where are my children?"

I was undoubtedly being very unjust, but the only thing that mattered to me was the safety of my children. Stung to the quick by my reaction, Vittorio decided to prove to me that he too was capable of moving mountains—and he succeeded.

The stratagem that he employed was extremely simple, but also dangerous. Instead of trying to be at all subtle, he went straight to the heart of the matter with a functionary of the German Ministry of Foreign Affairs. "Il Duce," he said, "wishes to reunite his family around him, and therefore he wants his grandchildren to return to Italy. I have come to get them." A request from Il Duce! Who but the Führer himself could refuse to comply? The German prudently decided not to lay himself open to trouble. He merely behaved as though he did not really understand Vittorio's project and gave him the gasoline necessary for the return trip. My mother was easy to convince and did not put too many difficulties in Vittorio's way.

The night following his departure from Germany, after a non-stop drive that was rather eventful because of the bombardments they faced en route, notably at Bolzano, Vittorio and the children reached the clinic at Ramiola where I was staying. Vittorio was immensely proud of having succeeded, and I was joyful at seeing my little ones again and extremely grateful to him. I shall never forget that, thanks to my brother, I was able to muster the necessary courage to face a new battle, the most difficult of all—for the deliverance of Galeazzo.

The first problem obsessing me was that of sending my children to safety in Switzerland. I knew that my hands would not be free until they were out of Italy and established in a neutral country.

Two friends, Tanino Pessina and Gerardo Gerardi, worked with me to achieve this end, which took one month.

Tanino Pessina, whose father was the owner of a large industrial cleaning establishment at Como (which Tanino now directs himself), and Gerardo Gerardi, whom we called Zio Piero so that the children could not reveal his true name, were in contact with an Italian who helped those with enough money to pay him to cross the border into Switzerland. I had no money, only jewels, and finally most of them were given to this man, including my diamond brooch given me by the King and Queen of Italy as a wedding present, a ruby bracelet, and a solitaire. But those jewels meant nothing to me compared with the security and freedom they could assure for my children.

When the agreement was concluded Emilio Pucci, another friend, who later had to pay for his fidelity, volunteered in turn to take my children from Ramiola to Milan, where they stayed for a day in an apartment with Zio Piero before being taken by him and by Tanino Pessina on the last trip of their flight. It was December 11, 1943.

The next day, December 12, I was informed by Pucci at Ramiola, where I had remained, that the children were now in Switzerland. He told me that everything had gone very well, except for the last moment when little Marzio, who did not want to leave Zio Piero, called out to him at the risk of alerting the frontier guards.

I was now going to be able to attend to my husband without any familial impediments to hold me back. Galeazzo had been incarcerated in the Scalzi prison for fifty-four days, fifty-four days during which we had seen each other only twice.

XX

It has been written that before entering his cell at Scalzi prison Galeazzo Ciano declared, "Prison for prison, I prefer to be here, an Italian among Italians, rather than in a German palace among Germans!"

It has also been said that Mussolini's son-in-law sang anti-Nazi songs in defiance of the S.S. guards who were rapidly placed before the door of his cell. All that is perhaps true, perhaps false. But there does exist one testimony that cannot be doubted because it comes from Ciano's prison companion—Zenone Benini, one of his childhood friends, as well as a former Minister in Mussolini's Cabinet. Benini spent several months at the prison in Verona because he had been in contact with certain members of the Fascist Inner Council who voted the Dino Grandi resolution during the night of July 24–25.

Zenone Benini's testimony is important not only because it allows us to understand Galeazzo Ciano's personality during his imprisonment better and describes the climate at Scalzi, but also because it has some interesting things to say about the mysterious person known as Frau Beetz.

"I knew on my arrival at Scalzi prison that Galeazzo Ciano was already there," Zenone Benini told me. "However, I did not see him for several days, and then, only after a strange visit I received in my cell.

"One afternoon I was drowsing, stretched out on my bed, when I heard the lock turn in my cell door. The door opened and a pretty, smiling young woman entered. Behind her a guard was carrying a cup of tea and a piece of cake on a tray.

"She spoke with a light German accent, but her Italian was perfect. 'Count Ciano has told me that you are a close friend of his, and he was so sorry to learn that you were arrested. He told me to tell you that you should not worry; he has not mentioned your name to a soul.'

"In fact, my only anxiety had been that Ciano or Cianetti had spoken of me. The day before the meeting of the Inner Council I had contacted Cianetti for Galeazzo to ask him if he were ready to vote the Grandi resolution. Therefore, by having me informed that my name had not been mentioned, Ciano relieved me a great deal. Moreover, as I discovered later, I had been arrested merely by chance. After Mussolini's return to power, during a conversation between Fascists at the Hotel Excelsior in Rome, making the rounds of all those who had been for or against Il Duce, Filippo Anfuso had said, 'As to poor Benini, we really have nothing with which to reproach him. What did he do? Insured contact between Ciano and Cianetti, that's all.'

"Pavolini leaped up, because anyone intimate with Ciano was suspect, and had me arrested.

"Several minutes after the visit of the mysterious blonde the door of my cell opened once more. This time it was one of the wardens, Mario Pellegrinotti.

" 'Your Excellency,' he said, 'come to the bathroom.'

" 'But I have no such need at the moment,' I replied.

" 'Never mind, come along,' he answered, staring at me strangely.

"So I followed him, extremely intrigued.

"The bathrooms were at the end of a corridor forming a right angle with that of the cells. Giving on to this corridor, there were several rooms serving as warehouses or depots. In one of them the former judge and advisor Gorini was lodged, and another was utilized for prisoners while their cells were being cleaned.

"Pellegrinotti pushed me into this latter room, saying, 'Be quick about it.' Then he walked down the corridor, as though he were guarding a prisoner who was in the bathroom.

"Before my eyes, arms spread wide, smiling, was Galeazzo Ciano.

"After having told me of what had occurred from July twenty-fifth until his arrest, Ciano said to me, 'There is no more hope for me. I have been dead since July twenty-fifth. But I don't really care: the Germans have lost the war, and that is all that matters to me.'

" 'And who is that woman who came to my cell?' I asked.

" 'A spy, but you can trust her, don't be afraid.'

"It is thanks to that woman that I was able not only to enter into contact with Galeazzo but also to follow the trial and to know, even before it ended, that there was no more hope—Ciano had to die.

"I learned later that the woman's name was Frau Beetz.

"Our position in that prison was rather paradoxical, for though we were always called 'Excellency' by our guardians, who treated us with the greatest respect, we could only leave our cell to go to the bathroom, and then accompanied by a guard at all times. We were comfortably installed—at least for a prison—and our meals were brought from a neighboring restaurant, but visits were extremely limited and all correspondence was censored in a very complicated manner. First, the pages were numbered and signed by the director himself. Then, once they were written, our letters had to pass before the prefect of the province, who examined them, had them copied, and sent them to their destination after making certain that they did not contain anything mysterious or contrary to instructions.

"We did have newspapers and were able to choose the books we wished to read in the prison library.

"Once a day we were taken outside for an hour's walk in a small courtyard. The only prisoner not permitted to do this was Galeazzo Ciano, who was also deprived of the right to talk—at least officially—with the other prisoners and to go to Mass. After several days' imprisonment he was even forbidden to receive the visit of the prison chaplain, Don Chiot.

"Aside from Frau Beetz, who was acting from selfish motives or perhaps because she was slightly in love with Galeazzo, the only person who attempted to soften Ciano's situation in prison was the deputy chief of the wardens, Mario Pellegrinotti. This was surprising since he was a noncommissioned officer in the Royal Militia and therefore thoroughly cognizant of the penal code, which he usually respected to the letter. But, as he explained to me one day, he had lived through the slow agony of so many other prisoners that he did not want to lose this occasion to show some humanitarianism toward members of the Inner Council, especially since he was well aware of what their end was to be. Then he added, 'You cannot understand what we feel when we must awaken a man at dawn and tell him that it is all over, that he must come with us, while he tries to understand what is happening. Even if the prisoner is an odious criminal, someone who has committed an unpardonable murder, you cannot avoid a shiver when you see him leave for execution and death after having watched him live for months, after having sometimes taken care of him, after having taught him to read and write, after having discovered who he really is, and especially after having said good morning and good night to each other, including the last night of his life.'

" 'Before I met him,' Pellegrinotti continued, 'I cordially detested Galeazzo Ciano. All the publicity surrounding him, the innumerable photos showing him posing with a jutting chin and arrogant air, all the gossip about him had finally made him seem terribly unsympathetic. But when I saw him I discovered an entirely different man from the one I had imagined him to be. He was courteous and patient, never lamenting his situation and inordinately grateful for the smallest favor. He never made any difficulties about the food, kept busy as well as he could . . .'

"Aside from those hours preceding the execution, the most moving hours in Verona were those at Christmas.

"Don Chiot had confided to me that he hoped to be permitted to have us attend Mass at Christmas. And finally, after many rebuffs at the Verona Prefecture as well as at the German occupation headquarters, he was able to celebrate the Mass at Scalzi prison on Christmas morning.

"It was strange as well as moving! There was a small table set up at the end of the corridor to serve as an altar. Don Chiot said Mass with only a nun from the women's section of the prison standing next to him to answer his prayers.

"As to us prisoners, we had remained in our cells, but we had been given permission to leave our doors ajar—and that is what made it so strange: the priest's voice rose between the walls, and the men in their cells were united in one single thought turned toward the Lord. It was as though there were neither doors nor walls, as I felt at one with the others sharing my fate.

"After the Mass, Don Chiot visited all the cells except for that of Galeazzo Ciano, whose door remained closed. By order of the authorities, he was granted no visit, not even that of his wife!"

Such severity was, after all, astonishing. Ciano was no different from the five other members of the Inner Council imprisoned along with him, accused of having betrayed Il Duce in voting the Grandi resolution. He was not accused of anything else, and thus should have been given the same treatment as his companions. But Mussolini, to whom his daughter Edda complained about this excessive severity, replied that exceptional measures had been taken concerning Ciano for his own protection, because they feared an assassination attempt by one or another fanatic.

Fanaticism, however, was the obstacle against which Edda Ciano stumbled each time that she tried to intervene in her husband's favor.

XXI

In fact, fanaticism was not my only enemy. I also was obliged to struggle against human fraility, against that jealousy which feasts on the sight of a young, handsome, intelligent man locked up in a cell, against the sordid political calculation that insists that one always be on the side of the strongest, against the instinct to do evil because goodness is a sign of weakness in some people's eyes.

Whether because of fanaticism, weakness, or whatever, the result was the same for me. After the twenty-third or twenty-fourth of October, I saw my husband's predicament worsen as the days passed.

First of all, there was the matter of the *Corriere della Sera*. During Badoglio's reign that newspaper had reprinted several times an article concerning the supposed fortune amassed by my husband. The piece was entirely false, yet it had profoundly shocked Galeazzo when it appeared several days after my father's arrest, while we were still in Italy.

Galeazzo had done as much as possible to defend his honor as well as that of his father. But as long as my father was out of power Galeazzo's attempts came to nothing, even though he wrote directly to Badoglio, the head of the government.

When Il Duce was freed my husband asked him to intervene with the newspaper to establish the truth. On November 25 he wrote to my father from prison, begging him to publish a denial in *Corriere della Sera*, and he obtained satisfaction without the least difficulty.

Following this affair of the *Corriere della Sera* there was another battle to be won, a battle much more important, for it concerned the liberty and the life of my husband. There too, I saw people's duplicity, weakness, stupidity when all those to whom I applied for help took refuge behind all sorts of excuses and, like the Germans, never answered my questions.

The only person who could do something was my father. At least that is what I thought. But it was difficult to reach him. Everyone, including my own family, counseled me against bothering him with the Ciano problem. How easy everything would have been if I could have turned my back on the situation. But I was unable to lie, I believed in the truth and in my husband's innocence, and nothing, save proof of another truth—which no one gave me—could have made me change my attitude.

My father would certainly have preferred simply not to see me rather than to have me speak always about the same subject— Galeazzo Ciano. After his words of encouragement during the first few days, and his sincere astonishment followed by his promise to intervene when I had explained to him the inhuman and inexplicable conditions in which my husband was being detained, the satisfactory conversations we had had changed into conversations that irritated him, because I began to fight for Ciano tooth and nail. I even believe that if he had been informed, toward the end, that I had been killed, he would have heaved a sigh of relief, despite his affection for me.

Thus, as the weeks passed, I discovered that I must renounce any hope of attaining something for Galeazzo from my father, especially since everything I told him was immediately known to the Germans. The men working for Rahn, the German Ambassador, and those under General Karl Wolff, who was chief of the S.S. in Northern Italy, had control over everything at Gargnano. They screened visits, telephone communications went through their exchange, their agents were informed about everything that occurred, and this to such a point that one day my father was obliged to make a terrible fuss so that there would no longer be S.S. guards stationed before the door of the Villa delle Orsoline, where his Presidential office was located, and that my mother had to lose her temper in order to force the S.S. men stationed at my parents' residence to leave her in peace.

I had been given a chance to notice this constant surveillance by the Germans. During one of my earliest conversations with my father concerning my husband I had said, "What is all this about there being difficulties in getting Galeazzo out? With only several determined men, I myself could see to it that he escaped from Scalzi, and with very little trouble!"

Several days later surveillance over Galeazzo, which had been insured by Italians—as for all the other prisoners in Verona—was handed over to the S.S. Two of them stood continuously before his cell, barring passage to anyone not carrying an authorization from the Gestapo to see him. Even Judge Cersosimo was obliged to request this authorization in order to interrogate my husband.

After the war certain newspapers wrote that those S.S. guards had been requested by my father after my visit because he did not trust me.

In short, despite my attempts, my support of my husband soon became merely epistolary. I was able to visit him only one other time before his trial and his execution: on the twelfth of December, the very day on which my children succeeded in crossing the

Swiss frontier. I still recall his happy smile when I whispered to him during our farewell embrace, "It's done, the children are safe."

That was our sole victory. I sincerely believed, as did Galeazzo, that we would be able to win another—which would allow him to recover his freedom.

There were several attempts made to free Galeazzo, but none of them succeeded.

The first attempt was made by Renato Tassinari, the Fascist prefect who was the head of my father's private secretariat during the Social Republic, who decided, along with my cousin Vito Mussolini, to intervene with Il Duce.

"After many difficulties," Tassinari told me, "we succeeded in seeing Il Duce and revealed to him our plan to assemble several resolute Fascists and to liberate Galeazzo Ciano, without Il Duce being officially informed of it.

"Mussolini listened; then, without saying what he thought of our idea, he gave me a short note addressed to the Federal Secretary of the party in Milan. In that missive he wrote: 'Please listen to what the gentleman bearing this has to say and then help him.'

"I went to see Giampeoli, who was very ill at the time, and I explained the plan to him. He approved it, and so we began to search for the men who could help in this mission. Everything would have worked out perfectly if Pavolini had not been informed of our preparations. He immediately intervened, and violently, I might add, and caused the operation to fail.

"Not long afterward we again intervened with Il Duce, and this time I had the impression that we were more convincing, because he had a definite reaction. 'I agree,' he said. 'I shall intervene directly in favor of Ciano if the Ministers of the government unanimously request me to do so in favor of a former Minister. I will not budge, except on that condition.'

"A Ministerial Council was held in secret. Il Duce posed the following question: 'Do you wish that Galeazzo Ciano and the other prisoners at Verona be freed or be pardoned?'

"All but three of the Ministers answered in the affirmative. The exceptions were: Mezzasoma, Minister of Culture and of Information, Buffarini-Guidi, Minister of the Interior, and Pavolini, Minister and Secretary of the party."

I am aware that efforts doomed to failure are nothing compared to the consequences of that failure. But we realized that there was a man sitting alone in his cell who could not even talk with his fellow prisoners, a man perhaps telling himself that if he had been an Italian like so many other Italians, if he had not fought for peace, he would not be there vegetating in prison. The hope that he might have a chance to escape was like a breath of fresh air given to a man who was stifling.

I have often thought back on those three months of agony that my husband endured. I know that Galeazzo was aware that he had no chance to escape his lot, but, in spite of everything, he proved to be a man of exemplary courage who not only inspired respect among the personnel and prisoners at Scalzi, but was for me a source of aid and comfort.

To return to the fight to liberate Galeazzo, there was finally the idea of my husband's escape in exchange for his notebooks, which the Germans very much desired to have in their possession.

It has been said that the person most active in this operation, set up by Kaltenbrunner and Himmler in order to cause Ribbentrop's downfall, was Frau Beetz. That is correct. But I must add that Frau Beetz was also the shining example of loyalty during this episode, in fact, loyal to the point of failing in her mission rather than betraying my trust.

People have claimed that Frau Beetz behaved as she did because she was in love with Galeazzo. Certainly, but of what importance were feelings—or my reactions to this—when the life of my husband was at stake?

Today I can say the same thing that I said at the time: Frau Beetz was what she was, but she never betrayed me. She gave my husband the letters that I wrote to him, she delivered to me those he wrote me, she gave Galeazzo the poison I had procured from a doctor so that he might escape the consequences of the trial and that he utilized—without any result—several hours before his execution. I do not know if the doctor had deceived me or whether Frau Beetz had given him something less deadly instead, but just as my husband took it without hesitation, so I would not hesitate to procure it if it were necessary to do over again.

It was Frau Beetz who came to see me when I ran up against a categorical no with regard to visiting my husband in Verona on Christmas Day. It was she to whom I passed the small gifts I had brought for him. She thus gave him the satisfaction of knowing that I had been only several meters away from him, thinking of him.

As to operation "last chance," it passed off in the following manner.

On December 26, 1943, I went once again to Gargnano. I did not intend to beg but rather to fight to the finish, my back to the wall, for Frau Beetz had informed me the previous day that the trial was imminent and that my father did not seem disposed toward the least clemency. Had she told me this to prepare me for her superiors' plans, which she was later to reveal? I do not know, but I was determined to do anything and everything as I entered my father's office.

When he told me that he could do nothing for my husband and that justice must follow its course, my reaction resembled that of one of the ancient Furies.

Beating the table with my fist, I threw at my father all I thought of him, his attitude, his German allies—whom I considered now as traitors and enemies after having been their most faithful and loyal of allies—and, disregarding what he must have been feeling if he really had been forced to bend before the exigencies of the Fascist extremists, I shouted my contempt and my disgust.

Before slamming the door, I remember having shouted, "You are all crazy! It's useless to have any illusions; the war is lost! The Germans will give up within several months. You know how much I once hoped for their victory, but now all is lost! Can't you see how ridiculous it is that Galeazzo should be condemned under such circumstances? We will be together again; we will be together again!"

I left immediately for Ramiola and, taking my husband's notebooks with me, drove to Como accompanied by Emilio Pucci. I entrusted the documents to Tanino Pessina so that they might be placed in security near the frontier, where I would pick them up when I crossed the border into Switzerland. I now realized that there was nothing more to be done in Italy and that I had to flee my country to play my last card—blackmail—in neutral territory.

That same night, December 26, I was en route back to Ramiola. The next day, still accompanied by Emilio Pucci, I left for Verona, this time to meet with Frau Beetz. I wished to use her as an intermediary to inform Galeazzo of my plan before I put it into execution.

At noon we were in Verona at the appointed rendezvous. Frau Beetz arrived and gave me a letter from Galeazzo. She also told me that the Germans had decided to liberate Galeazzo in exchange for his notebooks, insisting at the same time that the initiative had come from her alone. But I later learned that General Harster, commander of the S.S. at Verona, had received a coded telegram from Kaltenbrunner, his immediate superior, sent in Himmler's name.

My husband's letter, which confirmed what Frau Beetz had told me, gave me a shock, but one which did not last very long. I did not understand at first how Galeazzo could exchange his most prized possession, which he had wished to use as his justification vis-à-vis history, for his freedom. But he explained to me that he had decided, for one last time, to trust certain Germans whose aim it was to negotiate with the Allies, which he himself had always advocated.

I understood his reasoning, and also, in reading his letter, I realized that I did not have the right to object to the fact that a forty-year-old man wanted to live. Therefore, I decided to follow his instructions to the letter.

Emilio Pucci and I returned to Ramiola to await the sequel to

Frau Beetz's plan as she had explained it. On the third of January, 1944, while Pucci was in Florence on personal business, Frau Beetz came to see me in Ramiola. She brought me two letters.

In the first, written with the consent of the Germans, who thus were aware of its contents, my husband specified the following points: 1) I was to leave on the following day at dawn for Rome in a Gestapo car; 2) On January 7 I would find my husband at 9:00 P.M., ten kilometers out on the Verona-Brescia road. I myself would pass the frontier into Switzerland, while my husband would arrive there later, after having been "kidnapped" and then crossing through Hungary and Turkey, I believe.

In the second letter, written without the knowledge of the Germans, Galeazzo stressed that I must recover those documents still in the possession of Zio Gino in Rome. These papers were assembled in volumes covered with green leather and entitled "Conversations," while there were others on whose cover was written "German." I was to give the Gestapo officer who accompanied me to Rome only the "Conservations," which were to serve as proof of the value of the other documents in my husband's possession. Our aim would be achieved if those papers were judged satisfactory.

Since I was unwell, Pucci dedicated himself to helping us once again. He left for Rome with Frau Beetz in the Gestapo car, furnished with a letter signed by me and addressed to Zio Gino.

What he gave to the Germans was obviously deemed interesting, because I was informed that everything had gone well and that the January 7 rendezvous had been confirmed.

I now had to recover the notebooks, which were the essential guarantee for Galeazzo's liberation. However, they were near Como, at the home of Tanino Pessina, and Emilio Pucci, whose car had broken down, did not arrive at Ramiola until early in the morning of January 7.

That same night I had to be at the rendezvous. We left immediately for Como. By 7:00 P.M. we had reached the entrance to the

Milan-Brescia autoroute, going toward Verona. But our problems were just beginning.

Midway from Brescia the back tires went flat. It was about 8:00 P.M., which meant that I had only an hour to reach our rendezvous.

Pucci and I decided to separate. He remained with the car, keeping some of the documents, while I took the notebooks, which were to be handed over to the Germans, attaching them to my waist with a belt. I did not take all the volumes because they would have weighed too much.

We hailed a car and it stopped. The driver told me that he was going only to Brescia, but he permitted me to get in. There were two Fascist government Ministers in the car, but they did not recognize me since there was very little light. What would they have thought if they had known that the exhausted woman muffled up in her furs was Edda Ciano, whom the Italian and German police were hunting down!

It was impossible to find a car at Brescia. I began to run down the road, stumbling over stones, turning my ankles, falling, but always clutching the notebooks.

Finally I saw a German military convoy coming toward me. I stood in the middle of the road, waving my arms to oblige the first truck to stop and pick me up. When the Germans dropped me off, I stopped a bicyclist and told him some complicated story of a sick mother or a military fiancé whom I had to see in Verona. He took me with him and that helped me to advance several kilometers, during which, I might add, he proposed that I accompany him to his place.

At 11:00 P.M. I was waiting at the milestone ten kilometers from Verona. But I had arrived two hours too late—no one was there!

I huddled in the ditch beside the road protecting myself as well as I could from the cold. Each time a car passed I raised my head, each time I had the same mad hope, each time the same bitter dis-

229

appointment. I had to remain in the ditch until morning because of the curfew imposed by the Germans.

At five o'clock in the morning, frozen, filthy, exhausted, I saw two men fixing a flat tire on their car. I approached them and they looked very surprised indeed to see an apparition such as myself with my fur coat full of mud, my hair completely disheveled, my shoes a mess. I must have resembled a phantom in the morning mist.

I repeated the same story of a trip I had to make to Verona and asked them to take me with them. They agreed and, for the first time in twenty-four hours I felt a bit of warmth as I sat between the two men. I began to feel so good that I did not immediately realize that the driver had his hand on my knee. I told him that I was extremely tired and he was not insistent.

At Verona I had them drop me off at the station, at which I waited for an hour before going to the Kommandantur. It was probably mad to go there, but I had to find out what had happened.

At the Kommandantur, where I introduced myself as Emilia Santos, I asked to see General Harster, who had been put in charge of the Ciano operation. After having been given the runaround for quite some time I ended by giving my real name. General Harster then saw me immediately. I had been there only a few minutes when Frau Beetz arrived. She stared at me, incredulous and panic-stricken; then, taking me by the arm, she rushed me out into the street, whispering, "You are crazy to have come here."

She then told me simply that her superiors had changed their minds about freeing Ciano. Later, in her hotel room, she told me what had really occurred. Everything had taken place as planned until early in the afternoon of January 6. The two S.S. men responsible for the operation had arrived from Holland and had already donned their Italian officers' uniforms. They were preparing to make contact with their colleagues who were guarding my husband's cell, when General Harster received a telephone call from Berlin.

He had immediately recognized the voice that was giving, or

rather that was shrieking instructions from the other end—it was the Führer himself.

I must make a momentary digression here to say that I myself have never believed Frau Beetz's version of what finally happened. On the contrary, my feeling is that the Germans never intervened in this dramatic affair so as to obtain my husband's head.

According to her, Hitler gave Harster the order to stop "operation Count" instantly. The Führer even added, she claimed, that I was to be Harster's responsibility. In a word, I was to be immobilized so as not to be an obstacle and the notebooks were to be recovered no matter what the cost.

Frau Beetz could have taken the notebooks then, if she had wished, because she knew that I had them on my person. But she did not do so and, before leaving me, she gave me a letter from my husband, at the same time informing me that all hope was lost and that Galeazzo would surely be executed.

Upon my return to Ramiola I broke down completely. I was haunted by the spectacle of poor Galeazzo left without hope after the last few days of cheerful expectation, of Galeazzo who had nothing left save his courage to face the execution squad! But I had to recover quickly and resume my battle to save the notebooks, to revenge myself for the horrible assassination of Galeazzo that now seemed inescapable.

I decided to go to Switzerland, first in order to stake everything on one last attempt with my father and with the Führer by sending them both letters that my friend Emilio Pucci would have delivered once I had passed the frontier, at which point they could no longer touch my children or me or the notebooks; and then so as to be with my children as my husband had requested of me several times.

I reached Como on January 8, but this time I had to hide because I was afraid of being followed. In Ramiola I had been obliged to tack a paper to my door saying that I had taken a large dose of sleeping tablets and did not want to be disturbed, so as to be able to leave; and during the night I had climbed out through an open window. I deposited with a faithful friend and doctor a package containing the documents that I did not wish to take with me, along with some personal papers. I kept only the notebooks, still attached to my belt.

On the night of the eighth, in the company of Pucci, Tanino Pessina, and the person responsible for getting the Ciano family into Switzerland, Zio Piero, I slept at the Hotel Madonnina in the little village of Viggiu, near the Swiss frontier. Zio Piero spent the night negotiating my passage.

At the last minute, upon learning who I was, my "guide" in charge of getting me past the frontier demanded a sack of rice in addition to the money for the Swiss. I don't know how Zio Piero found the rice, but he did.

At the hotel I wrote the letters to Hitler and to my father, and then I wrote a third one addressed to General Harster. Those letters are now in the public domain.

At 5:00 P.M., on January 9, I left the hotel to draw nearer to the Swiss frontier. Emilio Pucci gave me a loaded revolver that I was to keep until my return to freedom. For, although I believed that freedom awaited me once I had crossed the border, I was in reality going toward almost total captivity, but that is another story.

Night had almost fallen when, having left my friends, I found myself with my "guide" several hundred meters from the Swiss frontier. I had to cross over an open piece of land to reach Switzerland.

At the last moment my "guide" pushed me to the ground; a German patrol was passing by us. Then he said, "Go now!"

Instead of running, I crossed the moonlit field with tranquil steps, standing quite erect. I don't know why, but at that point I didn't care what might happen to me.

The Swiss customs inspector was expecting the Princess d'Aoste —that had been the name given him—and he was astonished and annoyed to hear me say that I was Edda Ciano.

Suddenly everything changed! There was a series of phone calls between this frontier post and Bern. I was obliged to spend the night there—another freezing night! Then I was sent to Neggio, a small town where my children were living. I was no longer alone. But in Verona, on that tenth of January, 1944, Galeazzo was fighting his last battle against himself, against anguish. It was to be the last day and the last night of his life.

XXII

The Verona trial was a proceeding *ad hominem,* instituted against Galeazzo Ciano, whose spirit was dominated by the fanaticism of a vendetta dissembling under the cover of reasons of state and a political trial. It was imposed on Mussolini not by the Germans, who preferred to let the Italians manage the affair among themselves, but by the Fascist extremists, that is to say, the most fanatical among them.

This is not simply an affirmation of Edda Ciano's but becomes evident when the preparations, the development, and the results of the trial are studied.

The aim of those who pulled the strings in this affair was extremely precise—to eliminate Ciano physically and to place Mussolini morally with his back to the wall.

The operation conceived by the Fascist extremists took place in three waves: the establishment of a juridical and legal framework to justify their "vendetta"; the trial itself and its judgment, with all the necessary preparation to insure that the former

Minister of Foreign Affairs did not escape death whatever the verdict of the special tribunal; finally, formulation of a plan to prevent Mussolini from receiving in time the condemned men's appeal for mercy.

First, the preliminaries. On October 13, 1943, the government of the Social Republic of Salo (the name of the town in which the Ministry of Foreign Affairs of the new Italian Social Republic had been installed by Mussolini) issued a decree setting up a special tribunal whose task would be to judge and punish the "traitors" of July 24. The decree had been written by Alessandro Pavolini, the new Secretary of the Republican Fascist party.

Four days later, on October 17, Galeazzo Ciano, who was living in a villa under house arrest at Allmannshausen, was informed that he was to return to Italy on October 19 and would be arrested on arrival. His children had been taken from him several days earlier by the Germans, who had put them in the care of their maternal grandmother, Donna Rachele.

On the fourth of November, two weeks after Ciano's arrest and imprisonment in Scalzi, the Italian authorities began to assemble certain persons who were to be judged along with Ciano.

The prefect of Verona, Cosmin, and the major of the Fascist National Guard, Furlotti, who was to command the execution squad on January 11, 1944, drove to Padua, where they took charge of four prisoners: Giovanni Marinelli, former Administrative Secretary of the Fascist National party; Tullio Cianetti, who had been Minister of Corporations under Mussolini; Luciano Gottardi, president of the Confederation of Industrial Workers; and Carlo Pareschi, former Minister of Agriculture and Forests under Mussolini. The order for their arrest, which was only made out on December 19, called their crime "accused of treason and assistance to the enemy . . ."

Edda Ciano said to me, "It is horrible to think that those men are dead only because my husband had to die. I have often been saddened by the thought of those wives who suffered because of us."

On the fifteenth of November the First Republican Fascist Congress was held at Verona. It was the first and the last, for Mussolini, who did not attend, discovered upon reading the minutes that the objectives of the Congress had been completely put aside to make room for a veritable prosecution, of unbelievable harshness, not only against the nineteen members of the Inner Council who had voted the Grandi resolution at the July 24, 1943, meeting, but also against Mussolini, accused of having wished to protect Galeazzo Ciano, his son-in-law. In fact, the aim of that assembly had been to define the Constitution, but Il Duce refused to call another Congress, saying: "The future of the Republic will be decided on the battlefront, certainly not in a conference!"

That episode revealed something extremely grave: that the Fascist fanatics had found Il Duce's Achilles' heel—Galeazzo Ciano.

From then on, Mussolini could take only one of two positions: confront the most fanatical elements in his party and impose his decision upon them whether it be merciful or no, or simply let things happen. He opted for the second solution.

On the twenty-fourth of November, the decree naming the members and the president of the tribunal was approved in a Ministerial Council meeting, after being presented not by the Minister of Justice but by the Secretary of the Fascist party, the same Pavolini.

On December 1, 1943, the special tribunal was officially installed at Castel Vecchio, and it decided that the trial of the members of the Inner Council would be held in the main hall, where the Fascist Congress had been held. Vecchini, its president, even had a room adjoining the hall made over into a bedroom for himself so that he might remain at Castel Vecchio without leaving it during the entire trial.

The trial began rather badly for the prosecution, for although the examining lawyer, Cersosimo, had already opened the inquiry, Pisenti, the Minister of Justice, committed an action that raised quite a furor. Very early on Sunday morning he went to Castel Vecchio and, using his authority as Minister, asked for all the documents held in the hands of the prosecution. He studied them in secret and then went directly to Gargnano, where he asked to be received by Mussolini.

"Duce," he said, "after reading with great care through the evidence existing against the accused I have been able to find no proof that the members of the Inner Council were in collusion with the King or with Badoglio. Not one single proof, Duce! Under these conditions, the trial is absurd!"

Mussolini remained silent for a moment, then he exploded. "You, Pisenti," he shouted, "you only see this trial under its judicial angle, while I, I must see it under its political angle. *Po-lit-i-cal!*

Reasons of state must prevail over all other considerations. And now we must continue straight to the end."

Up to this point Mussolini's position was understandable. A political party has the right to take a position, a tribunal may exist for traitors, and a head of state should be intransigent about principles.

But, though everything appears legal and logical as to principles, as soon as we enter into the domain of their application the most elementary rules of justice appear to have been flouted and trampled upon in a parody of a trial.

First, there were the arrests themselves. Out of the nineteen members of the Inner Council who had voted the Grandi resolution, some immediately took cover, hiding from Fascist reprisals in Italy or abroad, in Switzerland and in Portugal, as did Grandi himself, who was able to leave the country with all his family, using passports furnished by the Badoglio government. But the majority of them remained within reach of the Fascist police.

Nevertheless, only six were arrested. And out of those six members of the Inner Council who were to be judged at Verona, there were, aside from Ciano, only people of minor importance insofar as culpability was concerned, since Mussolini himself had told his daughter Edda that the real culprits were Grandi, Federzoni, Bottai, Albini, Bastianini; the others merely imbeciles.

Why were none of those men Il Duce mentioned on trial? And why had only those people been chosen who had remained at home, continuing to go to work, performing their functions until they had been ordered to resign?

Luciano Gottardi would perhaps never have been bothered if, after the establishment of the Republican Fascist party, he had not written to its new Secretary, Alessandro Pavolini, asking him to enroll him as a member and giving him his address so as to receive his party card.

Pavolini, astonished because he had believed Gottardi already safe in Switzerland, sent him an immediate response—police who arrested him.

Cianetti had begun to laugh when the police came to his home. "You are making a great blunder, my friends," he said. "Mussolini knows how it all really occurred!" He was still laughing when they put him in handcuffs, but he stopped laughing when he saw that he risked losing his head. Happily for him, he saved it.

Marshal de Bono had no friends in the new government. He was imprisoned at Verona at the age of seventy-seven.

This proves that the Fascist police did not have to hunt down traitors in hiding. Ciano's coprisoners and coaccused appear to have served simply as an excuse for the trial that was to serve as the means of executing him.

Among those who might have been arrested, there was one who was even called as witness for the prosecution; that was Farinacci, one of the first of the Fascist party Secretaries. More Nazi than Fascist, Farinacci had not voted for the Grandi resolution, but he had presented his own resolution, which was more violent and more hostile to Mussolini than that of Grandi.

However, he was never bothered by the authorities. This did not save him from an early death, nevertheless. After April 25, 1945, he was "liquidated" along with his mistress, whose only crime had been to remain in his company.

As to the trial itself, its legal bases for prosecution were not at all solid, as Pisenti, the Minister of Justice, had told Mussolini. During the two days of hearings not one single proof of guilt was presented.

The minutes of the meeting of the Inner Council might have served, for example, as irrefutable proof for the prosecution and the surest means of verifying the declarations made by the accused. Those minutes contained the remarks made by the members of the Inner Council before the vote was taken as well as those of Il Duce before and after the vote. Thus, it would have been easy to define the degree of culpability of the accused, or at least their avowed intentions, by using this document. It would not have enlightened the judges as to the ties that had existed between certain members of the Inner Council and the men who had overthrown Mussolini on July 25, but the special tribunal would still have held a highly important card to use as accusatory evidence.

Well, the minutes of the historic meeting of July 24, 1943, had purely and simply disappeared. Carlo Scorza, Secretary of the Fascist party at the time, replied to the visiting magistrate that, at the conclusion of the Inner Council meeting, Il Duce had taken the document with him. As to Buffarini-Guidi, who had participated in the meeting and who now served as Minister of the Interior in the new Fascist regime, he declared that the minutes had been burned after Mussolini's fall from power. Why? No one has ever been able to answer that question.

That should have given pause to the tribunal, but instead it disregarded the entire affair, declaring that verbal proof and newspaper clippings would suffice—newspaper clippings as the basis for deciding the life or death of a man!

Marinelli, deaf as a post, declared that he had not understood the discussions that took place before the vote. He had believed that since Mussolini had permitted the text to be put to a vote, he could vote for it.

As to Luciano Gottardi, he accused Mussolini of having misled the members of the Inner Council. And his deposition was a model of logical and juridical clarity. It can be summed up in several words: It was Mussolini who put the Grandi resolution to a vote; it was he who decided that the vote should be completely free, just as it was he who asked the advice of the members of the Inner Council concerning the text, which had been presented to him in advance by Grandi. How thus can those who exercised a right given to them by Mussolini be punished by him for having done so?

But Gottardi's deposition was no more taken into consideration than that of Ciano or the others. Furlotti, the man who was to be in command of the execution squad on January 11, 1944, was less subtle and even inquired why it was necessary to have lawyers, proofs, and hearings for people who had been traitors and deserved to be executed.

Another detail: When the six accused chose their defense attorneys, two of them were obliged to use an attorney appointed by the court—they were Bono and Ciano.

Bono did not know any lawyers, but Ciano's case was different. He had designated Luigi Perego of Verona, who refused, saying that he was sick, and the two others to whom Ciano appealed gave the same reply. Why were they in such a hurry to refuse to defend Ciano? Was it because his fate had already been sealed or because secret influences acted on the lawyers?

Wishing to prove the culpability of the accused by any possible means, and in lieu of proof, the court called certain members of the Inner Council who had voted *against* the Grandi resolution and had remained faithful to Mussolini. Their testimony was extremely circumspect, and it was impossible for the public prosecutor, Fortunato, as well as for the tribunal's president, Vecchini, to make them give any evidence that could have buttressed the prosecution's stand. Nevertheless, the trial continued, ending in the sentence known to history.

Apart from the substance, which the Verona judges treated in an amazingly free and easy manner, the form of the trial revealed not only a determined contempt for legal truth, but also a desire to humble the accused, to degrade them before killing them.

For example, on the morning of January 8, 1944, as the public, carefully chosen, began to enter the chamber, a Fascist officer discovered with horror that the seats reserved for the accused were rather high leather chairs. He immediately called on the military and had the excessively luxurious—to his taste—armchairs replaced by uncomfortable, half-broken, wooden chairs.

If supplementary proof of the true intentions of the Fascist extremists toward the six men who were tried at Verona were necessary, it would suffice to recall how the deliberations of the special tribunal's judges took place and what arrangements had been made by the militia placed under Nicola Furlotti's orders.

It was 10:05 in the morning on Monday, January 10, 1944, when Signor Fortini, Cianetti's lawyer, ended his defense speech. He was the last counsel to plead. A profound silence reigned in the chamber. Before the judges withdrew to reach their verdict, President Vecchini, as though giving in to a sudden impulse, turned toward the accused and said, "I ask the accused if they have anything to add." Everyone, except Ciano, shook his head negatively. Ciano raised his hand, then at the moment of speaking he let it fall again, saying quietly, "No, I have nothing to add either."

While the prisoners were led into a small room on the ground floor to await the verdict, the nine judges withdrew to a meeting room to deliberate. And it is there that fanaticism reigned.

On the table lay a wooden box and, beside it, a handful of white and black balls in equal number corresponding to the number of judges. The white balls signified life and the black signified death.

Before the voting began, one of the judges, General Montagna, spoke up and succeeded, with the aid of another judge, in convincing his colleagues to examine the cases of the accused individually rather than voting on the verdicts in a bloc. Another judge, Enrico Vezzalini, tried in vain to stop this procedure by violently declaring, "The only distinction to be made is to know who ought to be shot in the back and who full-face, and that is all!"

The first name on which the tribunal pronounced a verdict was that of Cianetti. From the box, the president took five white and four black balls. Cianetti's life was saved.

The second accused to be judged was Bono: five white and four black balls. His life too was saved. President Vecchini was becoming increasingly nervous.

The third was Gottardi: five white balls and four black. A third accused whose head was saved.

Judge Vezzalini suddenly rose and shouted, "You are in the process of betraying Fascism! You too should end up in court being tried as traitors! I propose a second vote, but remember what I have just said!"

And then something unheard of in the annals of justice occurred. One of the judges who had placed a white ball in the box, Riggio, murmured in a low voice, "I take back my favorable vote." The new vote was taken first on Bono, and this time there were five black balls and four white ones—death.

The arrangements made by the militia were quite simple: If the judges had pronounced a verdict recommending clemency, Galeazzo Ciano and his companions would have been killed, either in the courtroom itself as soon as the sentence had been passed, or in the police van taking them back to Scalzi.

This has been confirmed in two instances. The first confirmation comes from Judge Cersosimo himself as quoted in a book written by Metello Casati and entitled *1944—Il processo di Verona* (*1944—The Verona Trial*) published in 1973. When Judge Cersosimo was descending the staircase to enter the room where the accused were awaiting the verdict he saw one of the secretaries talking with Signor Perani, Gottardi's defense attorney. The secretary was whispering quite anxiously to Signor Perani, "Warn your colleagues. When the sentence is handed down, keep out of the way and lower your head. If they are acquitted, the Fascist guard will open fire on the prisoners—this is certain."

The second confirmation was furnished by Nicola Furlotti, the man who commanded the execution squad.

In 1967 the Italian journalist Gian Franco Vené succeeded in finding Furlotti, whom everyone believed to be dead, and he interviewed him. That interview, published in *L'Europeo*, in *Le Figaro*, and later reproduced in Casati's book, is a model of blind fanaticism, especially when Furlotti declares to Vené: "I was certain, even before the trial, that Ciano would die."

"Explain what you mean by that, Furlotti."

"Certainly. If Ciano had been sentenced to life imprisonment, he would have died during his transfer in the police van from the courtroom to Scalzi prison."

"Died how?"

"Killed."

"By you?"

"It had been decided upon earlier."

"And weren't you afraid?"

"Afraid of whom?"

"Of Mussolini."

"Mussolini would never have interfered in that affair. . . ."

And later, during the same interview, Furlotti admitted, "If the requests for clemency had reached Mussolini and if he had consented, I would not have answered for the Republican Guard. We were determined not to allow Ciano to escape. . . ."

In short, as Edda Ciano has declared, "There are moments when a man's destiny seems to resemble a wagon riding the rails. It rolls on and on until the end of the line, and it is impossible to make it leave the track."

Along with Mussolini, the only man who could have avoided this drama was Alessandro Pavolini, Ciano's friend and protégé, a man who frequented the same literary and social circles as Il Duce's son-in-law, who was sometimes called a snob and who, far from being a rough, uncultivated, bloodthirsty person, was a cultivated and brilliant writer and seemingly broad-minded. But this was true of him only till the day he awoke to the fact that the Fascist adventure he was living through would end in blood and death. From then on this intellectual's exacerbated fanaticism took on the determination of the ancient Romans. He was willing to die, yes he was more than willing, but it must be a heroic death, and before that occurred he wished to kill all those who had not chosen the same path as himself.

As Edda Ciano was to say later, "At bottom, he was consistent with himself to the end."

XXIII

It was 1:40 in the afternoon on January 10, 1944. Galeazzo Ciano was standing in the courtroom of Castel Vecchio. At that instant President Vecchini began to read in a low voice the sentence handed down by the special tribunal.

Bono, Ciano, Pareschi, Marinelli, and Gottardi were condemned to death. Cianetti was condemned to thirty years in prison—he had been saved by the letter he had addressed to Mussolini immediately after the meeting of the Inner Council.

Marinelli and Bono did not understand what the president had said. They turned to Ciano, anxiously asking, "What did he say?"

"Cianetti has managed to save his head," replied Ciano. "But we are done for."

Marinelli burst into violent sobs.

The condemned men were led back to the small room where they had awaited the verdict. They remained there for three hours. All of them wrote their requests for clemency during that time, save Ciano, who refused to sign such a request, since he did not want to give Mussolini the satisfaction of seeing him crawl for help.

They were then brought back to Scalzi prison, where Zenone Benini had just learned of the verdict from one of the prison guards, who could not hold back his tears.

"The sound of the key turning in my door tore me from the apathy into which I had been plunged by the news," Benini recounted to me thirty years later. "I turned around and there was Ciano, and behind him the prison director.

"I fell into Galeazzo's arms, sobbing.

" 'Ah,' he exclaimed in a playful tone of voice, 'I come to see you so that you can give me courage and you burst into tears! It is *I* who am going to be obliged to cheer *you* up!'

"I calmed down a bit.

" 'You're doing all right!' said Galeazzo, looking around my cell. 'You've even got an armchair!'

" 'Sit down,' I said to him.

" 'Oh no, you sit down. I shall have all the time in the world to rest,' he replied.

"I began to cry again.

" 'All right,' he said. 'I'll sit in the armchair. Now are you happy?'

"He stretched out his legs toward the small stove. He seemed to wish to savor these moments, to live them intensely.

"The prison director left us, saying that he would return shortly. The S.S. guard entered and said in German, 'Count Ciano, I give you my word as a soldier that I do not understand a single word of Italian. You can speak freely.'

"Ciano was extraordinarily calm. He told me that it had been some time since he had had any illusions about his fate and that he hoped he would be permitted to confess and take Communion, but that the Germans had refused to let him remain alone with a priest for fear that he would charge him with a mission or reveal to him some important secret. Frau Beetz was trying to get the authorization from her superiors, however.

"Then he spoke of his children, of his wife, who had tried everything under the sun to save him. He told me that after the verdict had been read, he had almost shouted to the judges, 'Your turn will be next!' but that he had held back so as to continue the line of conduct he had imposed upon himself—scorn.

" 'Think of how my family has disintegrated,' he murmured. 'Papa died in June of 1939, poor Maria [his sister] in September of the same year, and I shall die tomorrow, January 11, 1944. My mother will be alone. She will hear the news on the radio, poor dear.'

"The director returned after half an hour and tried to persuade Ciano to sign a request for clemency. Galeazzo continued to refuse.

"It was finally Cianetti who convinced him by reminding him that the requests of his companions were being held up since his was not among them.

"'That's true, I can't do that to them,' agreed Galeazzo. And so he signed."

Those requests passed through the hands of one Minister after another during an entire night, then from general to prefect, from government figure to party chieftain—no one wished to take the responsibility of signing them or rejecting them.

Clinging obstinately to his vengeful hatred, Pavolini searched desperately for a man who would agree to reject them without running the risk of sending them on to Mussolini, in reality the only one qualified to make a decision about the condemned men, since he was head of the government and of the state.

At Scalzi prison, the condemned spent the night together in Bono's cell. It was a strange night of prayer, of despair, and of vague glimmers of hope.

Profiting from a moment of inattention on the part of his companions, Galeazzo Ciano tried to kill himself with what he believed to be cyanide. But the capsule had no effect on him. Disappointed, he murmured, "So I must die twice, alas!"

The electric bell, which rang automatically each time that the gates opened, had been disconnected by the assistant warden so as to spare the condemned men any useless apprehension about visits having nothing to do with them.

It was nearly eight-fifteen at night when a rumor spread through the prison that Mussolini had convened the Council of Ministers and that it was already in session. Hope was rampant that Il Duce meant to put himself in a position to be able to accept the requests for clemency. Even Ciano dared be optimistic.

By eight-thirty, the condemned men were beginning to exchange rather gay comments about this and that. Only Mario Pellegrinotti knew the truth. He sat quietly. Ciano, who noticed Pellegrinotti's eyes filled with tears, winked at Zenone Benini so that he would notice how nice the assistant warden was.

At eight forty-five the condemned men decided to go to bed at nine, since, no matter what the regime, no one was ever executed before dawn.

It was 9:05 P.M. when a shout informed them that the prefect had arrived.

Each man closed the door to his cell in order to be alone with his unbearable anguish. It was the decisive moment—life or death.

Through the night Zenone Benini heard the steps as they stopped before each cell. The silence that followed each visit was heavy with implication—it meant death.

Then the words "Pardon him! Pardon him before you die!" were heard.

"No!"

The voice was firm. It was the voice of Galeazzo Ciano. And Don Chiot, the prison chaplain, was pleading with him.

"Pardon him! It is God's will; pardon him!"

"No!"

A group had formed in the corridor and a stooped, slightly built man left it to go to Ciano. It was Marshal de Bono, who proceeded to put his arm around Galeazzo Ciano's shoulders, looked him in the eye, then murmured, "Galeazzo, *I* have forgiven him."

Ciano gave a start, stared in turn at the old man, lowered his feverish eyes and said, "Then I also pardon him."

He immediately walked toward the exit, followed by his companions.

Various important personages were assembling on the firing range of Fort Procolo. Prefect Cosmin was nervously chain-smoking—he even continued to smoke later on in front of the corpses. He wished only that it be over quickly. Nicola Furlotti, who was in command of the execution squad, was also nervous. He too was in a hurry for the men to be dead, but had found, much to his fury, that the chairs on which the condemned men were to be shot were not in place.

When the chairs finally arrived and the men were seated in them, Marinelli shouted desperately, "Don't do it, don't do it! You are committing murder!"

Pareschi reminded Don Chiot that he wished his body to be enveloped in a shawl that he had given to the prefect.

Ciano called the prefect to him and repeated the desire that he had expressed in his will to be buried in Livorno next to his father and his sister.

As Marinelli twisted and turned in his chair one of the executioners said to him sarcastically, "Calm down, old man! You'll see, it will be nothing at all. . . ."

It was nine-twenty. One salvo, several revolver shots. It was over. The Verona trial had entered into history.

Some time later, Il Duce said to Don Chiot and to Father Pancino, a priest who was a friend of Edda Ciano, "In his manner of dying, Ciano revealed a grandeur that transcends us all."

He also said to that same Father Pancino, to whom he gave five million lire for Edda Ciano after he had sold his newspaper *Popolo d'Italia,* "It was for reasons of state."

"Il Duce never had a disobliging word to say about his son-in-law," Father Pancino told me. "One day he said to me: 'You know, I remain here in my corner, I give orders, but I cannot exercise any control over whether they are followed or not.'

"And, sounding exceedingly angry, he remarked about his daughter, 'They had better not think that they can do with her what they did to my son-in-law. Anyone who touches a hair of her head will have me to deal with!' "

Were Mussolini's remarks sincere or was he merely acting a part? Father Pancino is unqualified in his response: "After Ciano's execution and his daughter Edda's departure for Switzerland, having said in person and written what she did to him, Mussolini was a destroyed man, morally rather than physically spent. When he asked me to allow him to take Communion and to return to the bosom of the Church, it was the gesture of a lost man who had found his faith again and clung to it because it was his only mainstay, and also because he felt himself close to God. I believe that Mussolini was sincere."

XXIV

I WAS WITH THE CHILDREN IN THE CONVENT OF THE SMALL
village of Neggio, where the Swiss authorities had in turn placed
me under a sort of house arrest, when the news of Galeazzo's
death reached me.

The Italian Consul at Lugano, a friend of my husband's, told
me about it in the early afternoon of the third day that I was
spending with my daughter and my two sons.

"Countess," he said, with deep sadness in his eyes, "I regret to
inform you that your husband was condemned to death and that
the execution has taken place."

So the inescapable had finally occurred. I had known it would
turn out that way, but it is always difficult to accept the unendur-
able.

That same afternoon I took the children for a walk not far

from the convent, toward a hill on the top of which a handsome cross surveyed the horizon. I was strangely calm.

When we arrived at the foot of the cross I said to the children, "Papa is dead. They shot him. He was innocent."

That was all. Fabrizio and Dindina stared at me, petrified, their eyes filled with tears. At thirteen and eleven, children understand what the words *shot* and *dead* mean. But Marzio, who was only six years old, was seemingly unconcerned, letting his eyes wander aimlessly. I thought he had not heard or that he had not understood, that is until he murmured, "Mama, look! There's a flower, over there!"

Then he ran, bent down, picked a wild flower that had grown, God knows how, despite the bitter cold, returned and offered it to me with a sweet smile.

He too had understood.

INDEX